walking in England

First published 2009

Produced by AA Publishing
© AA Media Limited 2009

Published by AA Publishing (a trading name of AA Media Limited, whose registered office is Fanum House, Basing View, Basingstoke, Hampshire RG21 4EA; registered number 06112600)

Visit AA Publishing at theAA.com/bookshop

This product includes mapping data licensed from Ordnance Survey® with the permission of the Controller of Her Majesty's Stationery Office.
© Crown copyright 2009. All rights reserved. Licence number 100021153

ISBN: 978-0-7495-6300-4

A CIP catalogue record for this book is available from the British Library.

Managing Editor: David Popey
Layout and Design: Liz Baldin at Bookwork Creative Associates
Image Retouching and Internal Repro: Sarah Montgomery
Series Design: Liz Baldin at Bookwork Creative Associates for AA Publishing
Cartography provided by the Mapping Services Department of AA Publishing

A04132

Printed by Leo Paper Group in China

PAGES 2–3: *The view from Hallin Fell over Ullswater, Lake District National Park*
RIGHT: *Dovedale in the Peak District National Park*
PAGE 6: *Castle Combe in the Cotswolds*

walking in England

Discover beautiful rolling countryside,

the coast, national parks and

inspirational views

Contents

This superb selection of walks introduces some themes and characters that define the beautiful landscape of England.

Introducing England

England is a small country and at a pinch you could drive its length in a day. But that would do the countryside a disservice, as you would merely glimpse the range of its landscapes. This collection of walks is an introduction to some of that variety, with routes chosen from some of England's outstanding areas. Treat it as an overview, sample some of these walks and then explore further.

An Extraordinary Landscape

Every part of England has its own special appeal. The West Country has lush green hills, smugglers' bays and rocky sea cliffs, with a clutch of glorious cathedral cities to contrast with its picturesque market towns and villages. In the southeast, London's breathless pace and world-famous landmarks are the main focus – but even the capital's broad commuter belt has its own rural havens. To the west lie the delights of the hidden corners of Essex, Kent, Sussex, Hampshire, Dorset and the New Forest. The Cotswolds have a distinctive charm, based on the golden stone of its buildings.

For a unique and evocative experience, roam the low marshlands and enjoy the wide skies and abundant birdlife of the East Anglian fens. The great industrial cities of the Midlands and the North have reinvented themselves as hotbeds of culture and nightlife; and then there are the plunging valleys, open moors and isolated farms of Yorkshire to discover, the glowering peaks of Derbyshire, and Northumberland's rolling hills, border fortresses and empty, majestic coast.

The natural beauties of the Lake District in the north-west corner of the country, draw millions of visitors each summer to admire the drama of the narrow passes, soaring mountains, plunging waterfalls and serene lakes of this outstanding scenic area.

The Walks

This book includes a variety of walks, ranging from ambles to longer-distance trails. Some of the walks are exclusively on footpaths and include routes across farmland and meadows that can be gloriously muddy. Others are along surfaced country lanes that provide easy and level walking. Most walks will offer a combination.

Walks Through History and Nature

There are few other places in the world where, during the course of a day's walk you can pass from airy cliffs or sand dunes, through riverside meadow and fields to towering crag-bound lakes and mountains.

Humans have so shaped the land over the last 10,000 years that there are few places left that can be truly termed wilderness. Even the wild, barren moorlands of the north of England – which many people regard as wilderness – are only that way because they have been cleared of woodland and used for grazing since the Stone Age. The dimpled impressions in a clearing of the conifers in Norfolk's fenland mark the neolithic flint mines, which were among the first industrial sites in the country. That insignificant mound on a Peak District hill may be the last resting place of a Bronze Age prince, buried some 4,000 years ago. And those strange corrugations that mark some Midland pastures, or the step-like lynchets on the steep slopes of the southern chalk downlands, show where every available piece of land had to be cultivated to counter the threat of starvation in the early medieval period.

Wildlife

Many other areas remain treasured havens for wildlife, and the nature walks in this book give you a taste of what to look out for. Stroll among the ancient beech woods of the Cotswolds or try to spot an adder or a rare natterjack toad in the New Forest.

You may be surprised at the diversity that survives in England.

using this book

Information Panels
An information panel for each walk shows its relative difficulty, the distance and total amount of ascent. An indication of the gradients you will encounter is shown by the rating ▲▲▲▲ (no steep slopes) to ▲▲▲▲ (several very steep slopes). The minimum time suggested for the walk is for reasonably fit walkers and doesn't allow for stops.

Suggested Maps
Each walk has a suggested Ordnance Survey Explorer map.

Start Points
The start of each walk is given as a six-figure grid reference prefixed by two letters indicating which 100-km square of the National Grid it refers to. You'll find more information on grid references on most Ordnance Survey maps.

Dogs
We have tried to give dog owners useful advice about the dog friendliness of each walk. Please respect other countryside users. Keep your dog under control, especially around livestock, and obey local bylaws and other dog-related notices.

Car Parking
Many of the car parks suggested are public, but occasionally you may find you have to park on the roadside or in a lay-by. Please be considerate when you leave your car, ensuring that access roads or gates are not blocked and that other vehicles can pass safely.

Maps
Each walk in this book is accompanied by a map based on Ordnance Survey information. The scale of these maps varies from walk to walk.

map legend

→‑‑‑	Walk Route		Built-up Area
❶	Route Waypoint		Woodland Area
‑ ‑ ‑ ‑	Adjoining Path	🚻	Toilet
☀	Viewpoint	P	Car Park
•	Place of Interest	🅿	Picnic Area
⌂	Steep Section	)(	Bridge

Year-Round Walking

The north-east tends to be characterised by slightly colder weather. Easterly winds can blow in winter and snow is not uncommon. But there are long sunny days at any time of year. Fog can be a problem for walks, so be prepared.

Walking in the north-west requires little in the way of special equipment. Fog and poor visibility, which can occur suddenly need to be kept in mind. Always let someone know your route and go prepared for sudden poor conditions.

What the east lacks in rainfall, it often recoups in bitter winds. On coastal walks take special note of tide times.

Central England's clay soils produce dense mud in wet weather. Although this is one of the drier areas of the country, it is susceptible to flooding from river water, especially in the Severn Valley.

The south-west experiences warmer and often wet weather, with winds blowing moist air from the Atlantic, bringing early springs. Mist and low cloud can be a problem, especially on Dartmoor and Exmoor.

England's south-east has relatively mild weather, but is as prone to showers as the rest of the country.

ABOVE: Walking high on Kinder Scout in the Peak District National Park

Head through fields from this obscurely named village and back along part of the Cleveland Way.

Along the Coast at Robin Hood's Bay

Walking the coastal path north of Robin Hood's Bay, you will soon notice how the sea is encroaching on the land. The route of the Cleveland Way, which runs in a huge clockwise arc from near Helmsley to Filey, has frequently to be redefined as sections of once-solid path slip down the cliffs into the sea. Around Robin Hood's Bay, the loss is said to be around 6 inches (15cm) every two years, with more than 200 village homes falling victim to the relentless pounding of the waves over the last two centuries.

ABOVE: The sea gave people in the area a lucrative piracy trade in the 1800s
RIGHT: The rocky shoreline of Robin Hood's Bay

Robin Hood's Bay

For countless holiday-makers, Robin Hood's Bay is perhaps the most picturesque of the Yorkshire coast's fishing villages – a tumble of pantiled cottages that stagger down the narrow gully cut by the King's Beck. Narrow courtyards give access to tiny cottages, whose front doors look over their neighbours' roofs. Vertiginous stone steps link the different levels. One of the narrow ways, called The Bolts, was built in 1709, to enable local men to evade either the customs officers or the naval pressgangs – or perhaps both. Down at the shore, boats are still drawn up on the Landing, though they are more likely to be pleasure craft than working vessels.

In 1800 everyone who lived in the Bay was, supposedly, involved with smuggling. The geography of the village gave it several advantages. The approach by sea was, usually, the easiest way to the village; landward, it was defended by bleak moorland and its steep approach. And the villagers added to the ease with which they could avoid customs by linking their cellars, so that (it is said) contraband could be landed on shore and passed underground from house to house before being spirited away from the cliff top with the officers never having glimpsed it.

There was a settlement where the King's Beck reaches the coast at least as far back as the 6th century. Despite strong claims that Robin Hood was a Yorkshireman, no one has yet put forward a convincing reason why this remote fishing village should bear his name – as it has since at least the start of the 16th century. Legend is quick to step in; two of the stories say that either Robin was offered a pardon by the Abbot of Whitby if he rid the East Coast of pirates, or that, fleeing the authorities, he escaped arrest here disguised as a local sailor.

RIGHT: Heather growing along the coast at
Robin Hood's Bay

walk directions

1. From the car park, return via the entry road to the main road. Turn left up the hill out of the village. Just after the road bends round to the left, take a signed footpath to the right over a stile. Walk up the fields over three stiles to a metalled lane.

2. Turn right. Go left through a signed metal gate. At the end of the field the path bends right to a waymarked gate in the hedge on your left. Continue down the next field with a stone wall on your left. Again, go right at the end of the field and over a stile into a green lane.

3. Cross to another waymarked stile and continue along the field edge with a wall on your right. At the field end, go over a stile on your right, then make for a waymarked gate diagonally left.

4. Walk towards the farm, through a gate and take the waymarked track through the farmyard. Continue with a stone wall on your right, through another gate and on to a track that eventually bends left to a waymarked stile.

5. Continue to another stile before a footbridge over a beck. Cross the bridge, then bear right across the hedge line, following the waymarker, then diagonally right towards the next waymarker and a signpost for Hawsker. Cross the stream and bear right. As the hedge to your right curves left, go through a gap on the right and over a signed stile, walking straight ahead through the field to another stile on to the main road.

6. Go right and right again, following the footpath sign, up the metalled lane towards the holiday parks. Pass Seaview Holiday Park, cross the former railway track and continue along the metalled lane, which bends right, goes downhill, crosses a stream and ascends to Northcliffe Holiday Park.

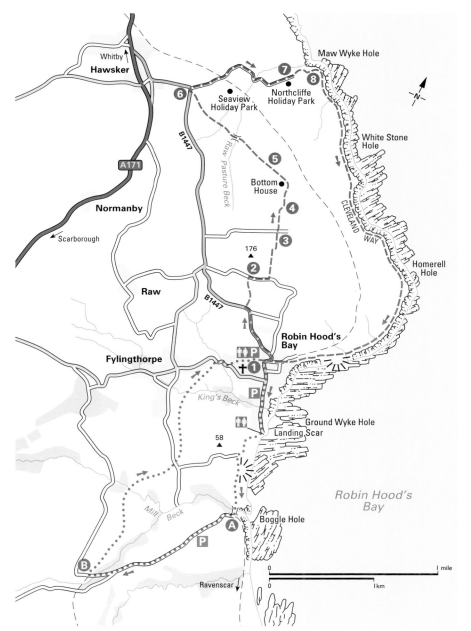

walk information

➤ **DISTANCE**	5.5 miles (8.8km)
➤ **MINIMUM TIME**	2hrs 30min
➤ **ASCENT/GRADIENT**	466ft (142m) ▲▲▲
➤ **LEVEL OF DIFFICULTY**	🖐🖐🖐
➤ **PATHS**	Field and coastal paths, a little road walking, 4 stiles
➤ **LANDSCAPE**	Farmland and fine coastline
➤ **SUGGESTED MAPS**	OS Explorer OL27 North York Moors – Eastern
➤ **START/FINISH**	Grid reference: NZ 950055
➤ **DOG FRIENDLINESS**	Dogs should be on lead
➤ **PARKING**	Car park at top of hill into Robin Hood's Bay, by the old railway station
➤ **PUBLIC TOILETS**	Car park at Robin Hood's Bay

7 Follow the Robin Hood's Bay sign right, and follow the metalled road, bending left beside a gate and down through the caravans. Just beyond them, leave the track to bear left to a waymarked path. Follow the path towards the coastline, to reach a signpost.

8 Turn right along the Cleveland Way for 2.5 miles (4km). The footpath goes through a kissing gate and over three stiles, then through two more kissing gates. It passes through the Rocket Post Field by two more gates. Continue to follow the path as it goes past houses and ahead along a road to reach the main road. The car park is directly opposite.

RIGHT: One of the narrow ginnels in the town

Extending the walk

After Point 8, follow the route to the main road, then turn left by the Grosvenor Hotel and walk down the steep main street of Robin Hood's Bay. At the bottom of the hill, just before you reach the shore at the Landing, turn right up Albion Road, signed 'Cleveland Way'. By Flagstaff Cottage, turn left up a flight of steps. The path ascends some boardwalk steps to reach the clifftop path. Where it turns left, through a gate, follow the Boggle Hole sign, still along the Cleveland Way.

Descend to cross the footbridge and ascend the other side. When you reach the metalled lane (Point A), turn right along it, leaving the Cleveland Way. Follow the lane, going right at a fork (signed 'Fylingthorpe'), cross the stream and, part way up the hill, turn right up steps on to the former railway track at Point B. Follow the line, which crosses a lane and eventually reaches a main road. Turn right along the road, and after 100yds (91m) turn left, signed 'Village Hall', which comes back to the car park at Point 1.

*A route from the magnificent ruins of
Fountains Abbey to the fascinating
medieval manor of Markenfield Hall.*

A Medieval Walk from Fountains

ABOVE: Some of the abbey's substantial ruins

After you have climbed the hill from the car park and begun the walk along the valley side, following the ancient abbey wall, the south front of Fountains Hall is below you. Built by Sir Stephen Proctor in 1611, it is a fine Jacobean house, with mullioned windows and cross gables. Were it anywhere other than at the entrance to Fountains Abbey, it would be regarded as a great house. Sir Stephen was, by all accounts, not the most scrupulous of men, having made his huge fortune as Collector of Fines on Penal Statutes. Nor did he respect the abbey buildings; he took the stone for his house from the south-east corner of the monastic remains.

Abbey and Abbot

A little further along the path, the abbey ruins come into view. When monks from St Mary's Abbey in York first settled here in 1132, it was a wild and desolate place. Nevertheless their abbey prospered, and became one of the country's richest and most powerful Cistercian monasteries. More remains of Fountains than of any other abbey ruin in the country. Its church was 360ft (110m) long. The other buildings, laid out along (and over) the River Skell, give a vivid impression of what life was like here in the Middle Ages. All came to an end in 1539 when King Henry VIII dissolved the larger monasteries. This was only a few years after Abbot Marmaduke Huby had built the huge tower, a symbol of what he believed was the enduring power of his abbey.

Mr Aislabie's Garden

Beyond Fountains Abbey are the pleasure gardens laid out between 1716 and 1781 by John Aislabie and his son William. John had retired to his estate here at Studley Royal after being involved – as Chancellor of the Exchequer – in the financial scandal of the South Sea Bubble. It is one of the great gardens of Europe, contrasting green lawn with stretches of water, both formal and informal. Carefully placed in the landscape are ornamental buildings, from classical temples to Gothic towers. The Aislabie's mansion stood at the north end of the park; it was destroyed by fire in 1945.

The highlight of the southern end of the walk is Markenfield Hall, a rare early 14th-century fortified manor house, built around 1310 for the Markenfield family. You can see the tomb of Sir Thomas Markenfield and his wife Dionisia in Ripon Cathedral. Open for four weeks in the summer, the house still clearly demonstrates how a medieval knight and his family lived; it is part home, part farm. You can see the chapel and the great hall. The gatehouse, convincingly medieval, is 200 years younger than the house.

RIGHT: An obelisk near Fountains Abbey
FAR RIGHT: Fountains Abbey was prosperous and powerful
until the 16th century

walk information

► **DISTANCE**	6.5 miles (10.4km)
► **MINIMUM TIME**	3hrs
► **ASCENT/GRADIENT**	328ft (100m) ▲▲▲
► **LEVEL OF DIFFICULTY**	🚶🚶🚶
► **PATHS**	Field paths and tracks, a little road walking, 3 stiles
► **LANDSCAPE**	Farmland and woodland
► **SUGGESTED MAPS**	OS Explorer 298 Nidderdale
► **START/FINISH**	Grid reference: SE 270681
► **DOG FRIENDLINESS**	Dogs should be on lead on field paths
► **PARKING**	Car park at west end of abbey, or at visitor centre
► **PUBLIC TOILETS**	Fountains Abbey visitor centre

walk directions

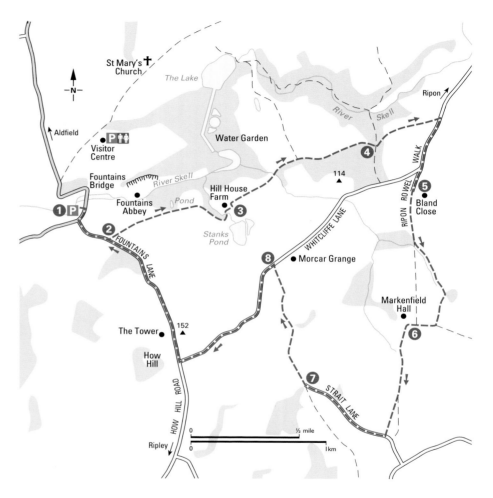

1 From the car park turn right uphill, signed 'Harrogate'. At the fork go left, signed 'Markington, Harrogate'. Just after the road bends right, go left at a footpath sign through a gate.

2 Follow the grassy path just inside the ancient abbey wall, and past a small pond. Go through a waymarked gate and follow the track as it curves round to the right through another gate, then bend left to a gate into Hill House Farm.

3 Turn right then follow the footpath signs to go left at the end of a large shed and then right. Go through a metal gate on to a track. At the end of the hedge, go ahead down the field to a gate into the wood. Follow the track, passing the ruined archway, to descend to a crossroads of tracks.

4 Go straight on, signed 'Ripon'. The track climbs to a gate with a Ripon Rowel Walk sign. Follow the track to a gate on to Whitcliffe Lane. Turn right. At the top of the rise go ahead on the metalled road.

5 Go over the cattle grid by Bland Close, then leave the lane to go straight ahead with the hedge on your right to a gateway. Continue along the waymarked track, eventually with woodland to your right. Follow the park wall through a gateway to reach a gate on to a lane. Turn right to reach some farm buildings by Markenfield Hall.

ABOVE: The remaining structures of the abbey have withstood time

6 Follow the wall to the left, going through a metal gate and straight ahead down the track, over a stile by a gate. Follow the track, then a waymark sign, across a field to a stile by a gate. Turn right up the narrow Strait Lane, to emerge into a field.

7 Follow the waymarked path beside the hedge. Go through a gate in the field corner and continue ahead with the hedge to the right. Go through two more gates. At a third gate, do not go through, but bend left through a hedge gap and down the field side, with the hedge on your right, to go through a gate on to Whitcliffe Lane.

8 Turn left and follow the lane, which leads in the direction of How Hill Tower, an 18th-century folly, to a T-junction. Turn right here and follow the road back to the car park.

Looking out for village mosaics and distant views on a quiet section of the Cleveland Way National Trail.

Out on the Tiles at Boltby and Thirlby Bank

The western boundary of the North York Moors National Park passes just outside the village of Boltby. It is a delightful, small-scale place, with a tiny 19th-century chapel and stone-built houses with red, pantiled roofs typical of the area. Despite its size, it used to have two pubs, as well as a tailor, a shoemaker, a butcher, a blacksmith and three masons. The single village street is crossed by the Gurtof Beck — pedestrians have their own ancient humpbacked stone bridge, from where the walk begins.

ABOVE: Heather and shrubs at Sutton Bank
RIGHT: A view across the Vale of York from Sutton Bank

Mosaic Trail

As you begin the walk you will notice a glittering mosaic of a kingfisher on a wall beside the Gurtof Beck: this is one of 23 on the Hambleton Hillside Mosaic Walk. This 36-mile (58km) route begins at the National Park visitor centre at Sutton Bank, and winds its way on and off the ridge. Further on in the walk you'll come across a tiled picture of a red-capped mushroom on a tree stump, and a search of Boltby village on your return will yield a dragonfly and a worm-eating mole.

Moat and Park

The farm at Tang Hall has more ancient origins than you might think. Just before you reach it, you will notice deep ditches beside the path, sometimes filled with water. These are the remains of a moat which once surrounded a medieval manor house on the site. A little further on, the parkland of Southwoods Hall is typical of the managed landscapes of the 18th century. There are fine beech, lime and larch trees, as well as a cedar of Lebanon.

Beyond Southwoods Hall, the walk passes through Midge Holme Gate and into woodland. This is very much pheasant country, and you are likely to flush out one or two of these noisy birds during the walk. Most characteristic is the male common pheasant, with its iridescent neck feathers of blue and green, its red wattles and long, arching tail. In contrast to the cock, the hen is duller – mottled brown and with a shorter tail. They are heavily protected from predators and poachers in these woods by gamekeepers, and kept well-fed during the winter months so that plenty survive for the shooting season, which begins on 1st October each year.

Fort and Lost

On top of Boltby Scar, just as you begin to descend from the Cleveland Way back to the village, are the scant remains of a Bronze Age hill-fort, one of several along the edge of the Moors. It was 2.5 acres (1ha) in extent, and surrounded by an earth rampart and ditch on three of its five sides – the others were protected by the cliffs. It was mostly destroyed by ploughing in the late 1950s.

walk directions

1 From the humpback bridge in the centre of Boltby village, follow the signed public footpath along the stream to a gate, and through three more gates to pass over a small footbridge to a stile. Continue following the stream; cross a gated footbridge, go over a stile and through a gate, then bear left over the stream and right to a gated stone footbridge.

2 Cross the bridge and continue over two stiles, then go straight on, beside the hedge, to go through two gates on to a metalled track at Tang Hall.

3 Turn left and, at the end of the farm buildings, turn right by a sign to Southwoods and through a gate to go diagonally left across the field; the route is marked by stones. At the end of the field, go through two gates then continue with a wire fence on your right. The path veers left and descends to a gate.

4 Continue along the track to a handgate. Go straight ahead on a track, confusingly named Midge Holm Gate. Follow the track to reach another gate beside a cottage, Southwoods Lodge, and go on to a metalled lane.

5 Turn left, following the track, signed 'Bridleway to Gormire'. At the signpost go straight ahead on the bridleway, up Thirlby Bank. This steep and often muddy track ascends the ridge; bear right at the fork part way up. Eventually you will reach a Cleveland Way sign on the ridge top.

6 Turn left and follow the Cleveland Way footpath for about a mile (1.6km) along the ridge, until you reach a bridleway sign to Boltby to the left. Descend to a gate then go straight ahead on the woodland ride, crossing a track to a gate. Continue ahead down the field, through a gate, and follow the track round to the right, along the edge of a wood.

7 At a signpost, turn right towards Boltby, to continue to a gate. Pass a tree stump with a mosaic of a toadstool and descend to a gate on to a lane. Follow the lane through another gate. Cross the stream by

walk information

➤ **DISTANCE**	5.25 miles (8.4km)
➤ **MINIMUM TIME**	2hrs
➤ **ASCENT/GRADIENT**	656ft (200m) ▲▲▲
➤ **LEVEL OF DIFFICULTY**	👭👭👭
➤ **PATHS**	Mostly easy field and woodland paths; very steep and muddy climb up Thirlby Bank, 4 stiles
➤ **LANDSCAPE**	Farmland, woodland and moorland ridge
➤ **SUGGESTED MAPS**	OS Explorer OL26 North York – Western
➤ **START/FINISH**	Grid reference: SE 490866
➤ **DOG FRIENDLINESS**	Dogs should be on lead throughout but can probably be off on Cleveland Way
➤ **PARKING**	Roadside parking in Boltby village
➤ **PUBLIC TOILETS**	None en route

a footbridge and continue up the metalled lane. At the T-junction in the village, turn left back to the humpback bridge where the walk began.

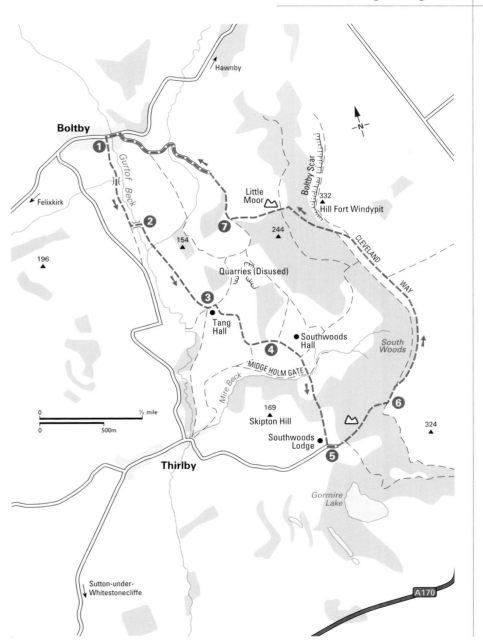

Walk from the shores of Ullswater to one of its most spectacular viewpoints.

Along Ullswater's Shore to Silver Point

ABOVE: The art of dry-stone walling continues in Langdale
LEFT: View over Ullswater from Gowbarrow Fell

The elongated hamlet of Patterdale has a rugged, mountain quality, providing the perfect contrast to the splendour of Ullswater, the southern shore of which lies hardly a stone's throw away. This walk strolls through mixed woodland and open aspect above the shores of the lake to visit the famed viewpoint of Silver Point. The adventurous may scramble to the top of Silver Crag, as did horsedrawn coach parties of old, for a better view of the lake.

Ullswater

Undoubtedly one of the loveliest of the lakes, the three legs of Ullswater add up to a total length of 7.5 miles (12.1km) with an average width of 0.5 mile (800m) and a maximum depth of 205ft (62.5m). It is Lakeland's second largest lake, not quite measuring up to Windermere. Its waters are exceptionally clear and in the deepest part of the lake, off Howtown, lives a curious fish called the schelly; a creature akin to a freshwater herring.

Apart from rescue and Park Ranger launches, you won't see many power boats here, but Ullswater 'Steamers' have three boats operating between Glenridding and Pooley Bridge during the summer. Alfred Wainwright (1907–91), known for his seven *Pictorial Guides to the Lakeland Fells*, regarded this to be a part of one of the most beautiful walks in the Lakes. Preservation of the lake in its present form is due to a concerted campaign, led in Parliament by Lord Birkett, against the proposed Manchester Corporation Water Act in 1965. Although the act was passed, and water is extracted from the lake, the workings are hidden underground and designed in such a way as to make it impossible to lower the water level beyond the agreed limit.

Among the trees, beside the shore, it was the golden yellow daffodils of this lake that inspired William Wordsworth's most widely known poem, *I wandered lonely as a cloud* or 'Daffodils' as it often referred to (published in 1807). His sister Dorothy recorded the event vividly in her diary: 'I never saw daffodils so beautiful. They grew among the mossy stones about and around them, some rested their heads upon these stones as on a pillar for weariness and the rest tossed and reeled and danced and seemed as if they verily laughed with the wind that blew them over the lake.' There is no doubt that this later helped William to pen his famous verse.

walk information

➤ **DISTANCE**	5.5 miles (8.8km)
➤ **MINIMUM TIME**	2hrs 30min
➤ **ASCENT/GRADIENT**	426ft (130m)
➤ **LEVEL OF DIFFICULTY**	
➤ **PATHS**	Field paths and tracks; some road walking, 22 stiles
➤ **LANDSCAPE**	River valley, wooded hillside and parkland
➤ **SUGGESTED MAPS**	OS Explorer 156 Chippenham & Bradford-on-Avon
➤ **START/FINISH**	Grid reference: ST 918682
➤ **DOG FRIENDLINESS**	Can be off lead on riverside pastures if free of cattle
➤ **PARKING**	Free car park on edge of Lacock
➤ **PUBLIC TOILETS**	Adjacent to Stables Tea Room in Lacock village

ABOVE: *The white exterior of the Patterdale Hotel at Ullswater*
LEFT: *Daffodils line the banks of Ullswater*
NEXT PAGE: *Pooley Bridge Boathouse, with its wooden balcony, on the shore of the lake at Ullswater*

walk directions

1 From the car park, walk to the road and turn right towards the shore of Ullswater. Pass the school to a track leading off right, through the buildings. Follow the unsurfaced track over a bridge and continue through the buildings of Side Farm to join another unsurfaced track.

2 Turn left along the undulating track, with a stone wall to the left, and pass through mixed woodland, predominantly oak and ash, before open fellside appears above. Proceed along the path above the campsite and pass a stand of larch before descending to cross a little stream above the buildings of Blowick, seen through the trees below. The path ascends again to crest a craggy knoll above the woods of Devil's Chimney. Make a steep descent, following the path through the rocks before it levels to traverse beneath the craggy heights of Silver Crag. A slight ascent, passing some fine holly trees, gains the shoulder of Silver Point and an outstanding view of Ullswater. A short there-and-back to the tip is worthwhile.

3 Follow the path, which sweeps beneath the end of Silver Crag, and continue to pass a small stream before a steep stony path, eroded in places, breaks off to the right. Ascend this, climbing diagonally right, through the juniper bushes. Gain the narrow gap which separates Silver Crag to the right from the main hillside of Birk Fell to the left. This little valley is quite boggy and holds a small tarnlet.

4 If you don't care for steep, exposed ground, follow the high narrow path to make a gradual descent south in the direction of Patterdale. But for those with a head for heights, a short steep scramble leads to the top of Silver Crag and a wonderful view. Care must be exercised for steep ground lies in all directions. Descend back to the ravine and the main path by the same route. The path is easy though it traverses the open fellside and may be boggy in places. Pass open quarry workings, where there is a large unfenced hole next to the path (take care), and continue on, to cross over the slate scree of a larger quarry. Bear right to descend by a stream and cross a little footbridge leading to the gate at the end of a track.

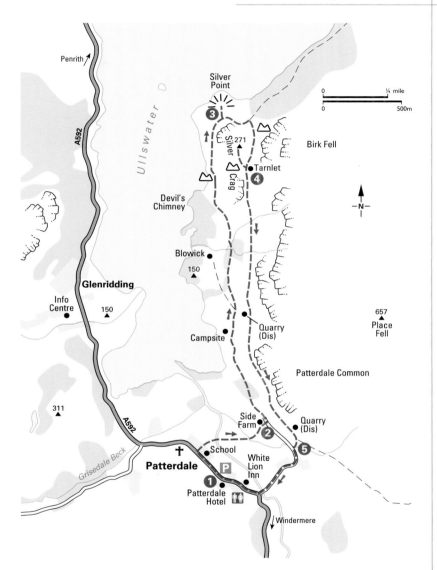

5 Go left through the gate and follow the lane which leads through the meadows. Cross the bridge and join the road. Bear right through Patterdale to return to the car park.

Bluebell woods, a lake, a tarn, a waterfall and
Little Loughrigg make this a memorable walk.

Four Seasons by Elter Water and Loughrigg Tarn

Elter Water and Loughrigg Tarn are among the prettiest stretches of water in the region. The former was originally named Eltermere, which translates directly from the Old Norse (Viking) into 'swan lake'. The swans are still here in abundance and are much in evidence from the wooden bench at the foot of the lake. The views over both lake and tarn, to the reclining lion profile of the Langdale Pikes, are particularly evocative. Although it does include steep sections of ascent and descent this is not a difficult walk, with outstanding views throughout.

ABOVE: *View of Loughrigg Tarn near Ambleside*
RIGHT: *Beautiful Little Langdale*

Each season paints a different picture. Golden daffodils by Langdale Beck in early spring, bluebells in Rob Rash woods in May, yellow maple in Elterwater village in October and a thousand shades of green, everywhere, all summer. The river is dominant throughout the lower stages of the walk. It starts as the Great Langdale Beck, before emerging from the confines of Elter Water as the sedate River Brathay. Ascent then leads to the suspended bowl of Loughrigg Tarn, followed by the open fell freedom of Little Loughrigg. This is very much a walk for all seasons, and should the section through the meadows by the Brathay be flooded, then a simple detour can easily be made on to the road to bypass the problem.

Local Gunpowder Works

With all the quarrying and mining that once took place in the Lake District, including a little poaching for the pot, there used to be a considerable demand for 'black powder' or gunpowder. Elterwater Gunpowder Works, founded in 1824, once filled that demand. The natural water power of Langdale Beck was utilised to drive great grinding wheels or millstones. Prime quality charcoal came from the local coppices, whilst saltpetre and sulphur were imported. In the 1890s the works employed around 80 people. Accidental explosions did occur, notably in 1916 when four men were killed. The whole enterprise closed down in 1929. Today the site is occupied by the highly desirable Langdale Timeshare organisation, with only the massive mill wheels on display to bear witness to times past.

Of course, the raw ingredients had to be brought in and the highly explosive gunpowder taken away. That was done by horse and cart. Clydesdales were preferred for their huge strength and considerable intelligence. On workdays they would be harnessed and on special occasions their manes would be plaited and ribboned and they were decorated with polished horse brasses. The horses have long gone but some of the brasses remain fixed to the oak beams in the Britannia Inn.

*LEFT: The Langdale Pikes rise above the trees and village of
Elterwater in the Great Langdale Valley
RIGHT: Loughrigg Tarn and Loughrigg Fell in autumn
PAGE 37: Langdale Pikes seen from Great Langdale*

walk information

➤ **DISTANCE**	4 miles (6.4km)
➤ **MINIMUM TIME**	2hrs
➤ **ASCENT/GRADIENT**	328ft (100m) ▲▲▲
➤ **LEVEL OF DIFFICULTY**	🥾🥾🥾
➤ **PATHS**	Grassy and stony paths and tracks, surfaced lane, 4 stiles
➤ **LANDSCAPE**	Lake, tarn, fields, woods, open fellside, views to fells
➤ **SUGGESTED MAPS**	OS Explorer OL7 The English Lakes (SE)
➤ **START/FINISH**	Grid reference: NY 328048
➤ **DOG FRIENDLINESS**	Under control at all time; fellside grazed by sheep
➤ **PARKING**	Trust pay-and-display car park at Elterwater village
➤ **PUBLIC TOILETS**	Above car park in Elterwater village

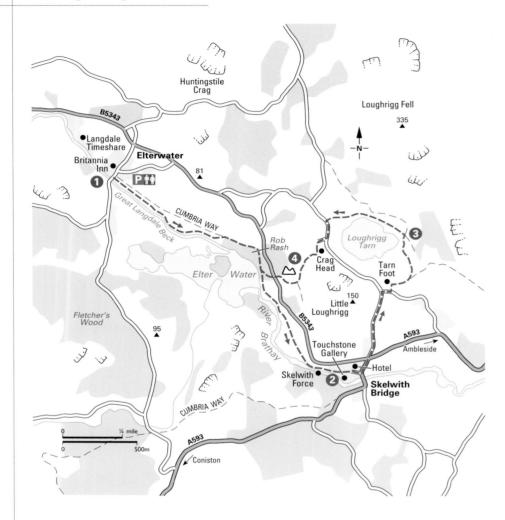

path through the meadows above the river. Note that this section can be wet and is prone to flooding. Pass through the gate and enter mixed woods. Keep along the path to pass Skelwith Force waterfall down to the right. A little bridge leads across a channel to a viewing point above the falls. Keep along the path to pass through industrial buildings belonging to Kirkstone Quarry.

2 Touchstone Gallery is on the right, as the path becomes a small surfaced road. Continue to intercept the A593 by the bridge over the river where there are picnic benches. Turn left to pass the hotel. At the road junction, cross over the Great Langdale road to a lane that passes by the end of the cottages. Follow the lane, ascending to intercept another road. Turn right for a short distance and then left towards Tarn Foot farm. Bear right along the track, in front of the cottages. Where the track splits, bear left. Through the gate carry on along the track to overlook Loughrigg Tarn. At a point half-way along the tarn cross the stile over the iron railings on the left.

3 Follow the footpath down the meadow to traverse right, just above the tarn. The footpath swings off right to climb a ladder stile over the stone wall. Follow the grassy track leading right, up the hill, to a gate and stile on to the road. Turn left along the road, until a surfaced drive leads up to the right, signed 'Public Footpath Skelwith Bridge'. Pass a small cottage and keep on the track to pass a higher cottage, Crag Head. A little way above this, a narrow grassy footpath leads off right, up the hillside, to gain a level shoulder between the craggy outcrops of Little Loughrigg.

4 Cross the shoulder and descend the path, passing a little tarnlet to the right, to intercept a stone wall. Keep left along the wall descending to find, in a few hundred paces, a ladder stile leading over the wall into the upper woods of Rob Rash. A steep descent leads down to the road. Cross this directly, and go through the gap in the wall next to the large double gates. Descend a track to meet up with the outward route. Bear right to return to Elterwater village.

walk directions

1 Pass through a small gate to walk downsteam above Great Langdale Beck. Continue to enter the mixed woods of Rob Rash. A little gate leads through the stone wall; the open foot of Elter Water lies to the right. Continue along the

Above little Ambleside, Loughrigg Fell
looks out to lake, dale and high fell.

Lilies and Lakes Seen from Loughrigg

ABOVE: *The stone Bridge House spans Stock Ghyll*
LEFT: *View from Loughrigg Fell, north of Skelwith Bridge*

Loughrigg is a delightful low fell, running from Ambleside and the head of Windermere lake towards both Langdale and Grasmere. This circuit walk crosses the River Rothay by Miller Bridge and rises to a craggy viewpoint before traversing the small Lily Tarn to return via the stone lane of Miller Brow. The views are some of the most evocative in the region. The delightful detail of tree, rocky knoll, heather, bracken and the white and green cup and saucers of the lilies on Lily Tarn, contrast with the grand open views of mountain, dale and lake.

Ambleside

Even before the heights of lovely Loughrigg are reached, the varied slate stone buildings of Ambleside provide an intriguing start to the walk. Indeed, despite recent developments, there is a lot more to this little town than just being the outdoor equipment capital of Britain. Sited in the old county of Westmorland, Ambleside has long been a site of occupation. Bronze Age remains, c2000 BC can be seen on the nearby fells and the Galava Roman fort, near Waterhead, was one of the most important in north-west England.

How Head, just up the Kirkstone road, one of the oldest surviving buildings in old Ambleside, is located in the area known as Above Stock. Sections of this fine stone house date back to the 16th century and it was once the lodge of the Master Forester of the Barony of Kendal. It has massive circular chimneys, a typical Westmorland feature, and stone mullioned windows. Other parts of its structure incorporate stone from the old Roman fort at Waterhead and cobbles from the bed of Stock Ghyll Beck.

Stock Ghyll once served as the lifeblood of the town when, some 150 years ago, it provided water power for 12 watermills. On this walk we pass a restored waterwheel, immediately followed by the famous Bridge House, one of the most photographed buildings in the Lake District. Spanning the beck, this tiny 17th-century building is said to have been built thus to avoid paying land tax. Locally it is said to have once housed a family with six children. It is now a shop and information centre for the National Trust. Ambleside has become a major tourist resort with shops, hotels and restaurants, and is a convenient base for exploring the rest of the Lake District.

RIGHT: A hilltop view of Ambleside
OPPOSITE: Hikers looking over Grasmere from Loughrigg Fell
NEXT PAGE: Lake Windermere with the village of Ambleside on the banks in the distance

walk information

➤ **DISTANCE**	3.25 miles (5.2km)
➤ **MINIMUM TIME**	1hr 45min
➤ **ASCENT/GRADIENT**	575ft (175m) ▲▲▲
➤ **LEVEL OF DIFFICULTY**	🚶🚶🚶
➤ **PATHS**	Road, paths and tracks, can be muddy in places, 3 stiles
➤ **LANDSCAPE**	Town, park and open hillside with views to high fells
➤ **SUGGESTED MAPS**	OS Explorer OL7 The English Lakes (SE)
➤ **START/FINISH**	Grid reference: NY 375047
➤ **DOG FRIENDLINESS**	Under control; busy roads, park, sheep grazing
➤ **PARKING**	Ambleside central car park
➤ **PUBLIC TOILETS**	At car park

walk directions

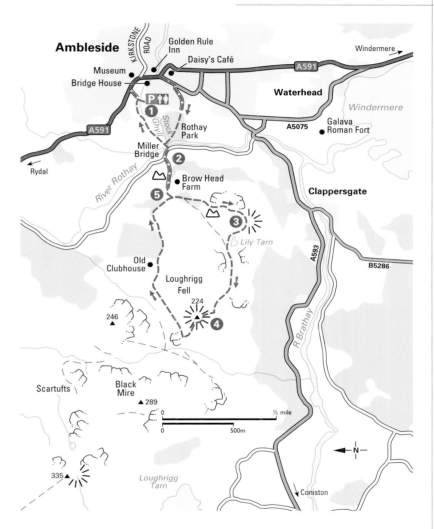

1 Take the wooden footbridge from the car park and go right, along the Rydal road, to pass the waterwheel and Bridge House. At the junction bear right along Compston Road. Continue to the next junction, with the cinema on the corner, then bear right to cross the side road and enter Vicarage Road alongside the chip shop. Pass the school and enter Rothay Park. Follow the main path through the park to emerge by a flat bridge over Stock Ghyll Beck. Cross this then go left to cross over the stone arched Miller Bridge spanning the River Rothay.

2 Bear right along the road over the cattle grid until, in a few paces, a steep surfaced road rises to the left. Climb the road, which becomes unsurfaced, by the buildings of Brow Head Farm. At the S-bend beyond the buildings, a stone stile leads up and off left. Pass through the trees to find, in a few dozen paces, a stone squeeze stile. Pass through this, cross a little bridge and climb the open hillside above. The paths are well worn and a variety of routes are possible. For the best views over Windermere keep diagonally left. Rising steeply at first, the path levels before rising again to ascend the first rocky knoll. Cross a stile and a higher, larger knoll offering definitive views of the Fairfield Horseshoe to the north and over Windermere to the south.

3 Beyond this, the way descends to the right, dropping to a well-defined path. Follow the path to pass a little pond before cresting a rise and falling to lovely little Lily Tarn (flowers bloom late June to September). The path skirts the right edge of the tarn, roughly following the crest of Loughrigg Fell before joining a wall on the left. Follow this down through a kissing gate and the base of a further knoll. This is ascended to another worthy viewpoint.

4 Take the path descending right to a prominent track below. Bear right to a gate which leads through the stone wall boundary of the open fell and into a field. Continue to descend the track, passing an interesting building on the left, the old golf clubhouse. Intercept the original route just above the buildings of Brow Head.

5 Continue to cross Miller Bridge then, before the flat bridge, bear left to follow the track by the side of Stock Ghyll Beck. Beyond the meadows a lane through the houses leads to the main Rydal road. Bear right on the road to the car park beyond the fire station.

A dramatic route to Kinder Downfall follows the famous trespassers of 1932.

In the Footsteps of the Trespass

If you want to climb one of the quieter ways to Kinder Scout, Hayfield to the west is one of the best places to start. It's also a route with a bit of history to it. From the beginning of the 20th century there had been conflict between ramblers and the owners of Kinder's moorland plateau. By 1932 ramblers from the industrial conurbations of Sheffield and Manchester, disgusted by lack of government action to open up the moors to walkers, decided to hold a mass trespass on Kinder Scout.

ABOVE: A plaque commemorating the mass trespass of Kinder Scout in 1932
RIGHT: View from Kinder Downfall towards the Kinder Reservoir

A Right to Roam

Benny Rothman, a Manchester rambler and a staunch communist, would lead the Kinder Scout trespass on Sunday 24 April. The police expected to intercept Benny at Hayfield railway station, but he outwitted them by arriving on his bicycle, not in the village itself, but at Bowden Bridge Quarry to the east. Here he was greeted by hundreds of cheering fellow ramblers. With the police in hot pursuit the group made their way towards Kinder Scout.

Although they were threatened and barracked by a large gathering of armed gamekeepers the ramblers still managed to get far enough to join their fellow trespassers from Sheffield, who had come up from the Snake Inn. Predictably, fighting broke out and Benny Rothman was one of five arrested. He was given a four-month jail sentence for unlawful assembly and breach of the peace. The ramblers' cause inspired folk singer, Ewan McColl (famous for *Dirty Old Town* and *The First Time Ever I Saw Your Face*) to write *The Manchester Rambler*, which became something of an anthem for the proliferating walkers' clubs and societies. However it took until 1951, when the recently formed National Park negotiated access agreements with the landowners, for the situation to improve.

Just like the mass trespass this walk starts at Bowden Bridge, where you will see a commemorative plaque on the rock face above the car park. After climbing through the Kinder Valley and above Kinder Reservoir you'll find the same moors of purple heather and the enticing craggy sides of the Scout.

The Downfall

Now you climb to the edge for the most spectacular part of the walk – the part that would have been a trespass all those years ago – and continue along a promenade of dusky gritstone rock. Round the next corner you come to the dark shadow-filled cleft in the rocks of the Kinder Downfall. In the dry summer months the fall is a mere trickle, just enough to wet the rocks, but after the winter rains it can turn into a 100ft (30m) torrent, thrashing against the jumble of boulders below. The prevailing west wind often catches the torrent, funnelling it back up to the top rocks like plumes of white smoke. In contrast, the way down is gentle, leaving the edge at Red Brook and descending the pastures of Tunstead Clough Farm. A quiet leafy lane takes you back into the Kinder Valley.

1 Turn left out of the car park and walk up the lane, which winds beneath the trees and by the banks of the River Kinder. After 550yds (503m), leave the lane at a signposted footpath after crossing a bridge. Follow the path as it traces the east bank of the river before turning left to rejoin the road at a point just short of the treatment plant buildings.

2 Here you fork left through a gate on to a cobbled bridleway, climbing above the buildings. It continues alongside the reservoir's north shore, turning sharp left on White Brow. Beyond a gate, but don't cross over the footbridge, follow the path instead as it climbs alongside William Clough, where it is joined by the Snake Path from the left.

3 The path crosses and recrosses the stream as it works its way up the grass and heather clough. In the upper stages the narrowing clough loses its vegetation and the stream becomes a trickle in the peat. Climb to Ashop Head where you meet the Pennine Way at a crossroads of paths.

4 Turn right to walk along the slabbed Pennine Way path across the moor towards Kinder Scout's north-west edge, then climb those last gritstone slopes on a pitched path to gain the summit plateau. Now it's easy walking along the edge.

5 After turning left into the rocky combe of the River Kinder, the Mermaid's Pool and the Kinder Downfall (waterfalls) come into view. Descend to cross the Kinder's shallow rocky channel about 100yds (91m) back from the edge before turning right and continuing along the edge.

6 Beyond Red Brook, leave the plateau by taking the right fork, which descends south westwards, contouring round grassy slopes beneath the rocky edge.

7 After passing The Three Knolls rocks and swinging right beneath the slopes of Kinderlow End, go through a gate in a fence (grid reference 066867) before taking a right fork to reach another gate in the wall dividing the moor and farmland. Go over a stile next to it and then turn left through a gateway. Descend the trackless pastured spur, passing through several gates and stiles at the field boundaries to pass to the left of Tunstead Clough Farm.

8 Turn right beyond the farmhouse to follow a winding track that descends into the upper Sett Valley. At the crossroads of lanes at the bottom, go straight ahead, and along the road to emerge at Bowden Bridge.

walk information

➤ **DISTANCE**	8 miles (12.9km)
➤ **MINIMUM TIME**	5hrs
➤ **ASCENT/GRADIENT**	1,450ft (440m) ▲▲▲
➤ **LEVEL OF DIFFICULTY**	👥👥👥
➤ **PATHS**	Well-defined tracks and paths, quite a few stiles
➤ **LANDSCAPE**	Heather and peat moorland and farm pastures
➤ **SUGGESTED MAPS**	OS Explorer OL1 Dark Peak
➤ **START/FINISH**	Grid reference: SK 048869
➤ **DOG FRIENDLINESS**	Walk is on farmland and access agreement land, dogs should be kept on leads
➤ **PARKING**	Bowden Bridge pay car park
➤ **PUBLIC TOILETS**	Across bridge from car park

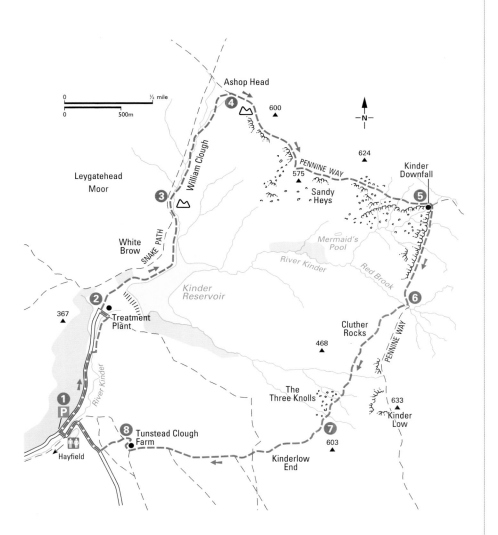

*A walk through the
alpine-like splendour of the
Peak's most famous dale.*

Dovedale: Ivory Spires and Wooded Splendour

ABOVE: *A tranquil tree-lined lake at Dovedale*
LEFT: *The view towards Bunster Hill from the
isolated limestone Thorpe Cloud hill*

Right from the start there's drama as you follow the River Dove, wriggling through a narrow gorge between Bunster Hill and the towering pyramid of Thorpe Cloud. A limestone path urges you to climb to a bold rocky outcrop high above the river. Lovers' Leap has a fine view across the dale to pinnacles of the Twelve Apostles. It's a view to gladden your hearts – not the sort of place you'd think of throwing yourself from at all. However, in 1761 an Irish dean and his lady companion, who were out horse riding (or were they horsing about?) fell off the rock. The dean died of his injuries but the lady survived to tell the tale.

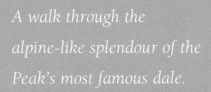

Spires and Caves

The Dove writhes round another corner. Above your head, flaky fingers of limestone known as the Tissington Spires rise out from thick woodland cover. Just a few footsteps away on the right there's a splendid natural arch, which is just outside the entrance to Reynard's Cave. This is the result of the cave's roof collapsing.

The dale's limestone walls close in. The path climbs to a place more remote from the rushing river, which often floods around here. As the valley opens out again two gigantic rock stacks face each other across the Dove. Pickering Tor has a small cave at its foot. A little footbridge allows you across to the other side to the foot of Ilam Rock. This 80ft (25m) leaning thumb of limestone has an overhang on the south side that's popular with climbers. It too has a cave at the bottom, which is only 4ft (1.2m) at the entrance but opens out to more than 30ft (10m) inside.

You will get a better view of them when you cross the little footbridge to the cave at the foot of the rocks. On this side you're in Staffordshire and the paths are less populated.

Hurt's Wood and Hall Dale

The continuing walk into Hall Dale heralds a less formal landscape. The dale is dry and it climbs up the hillside. Hurts Wood has wych elm, whitebeam, ash and rowan. Some fences have kept grazing animals out, allowing the trees and shrubs to regenerate. Hurts Wood is alive and well. You'll hear and see many birds – warblers, redstarts and black caps; and you'll spot wild flowers – dog's mercury, wood anemone and wood forget-me-not.

It seems a shame to leave the dale behind but soon you're walking down a quiet lane with Ilam and the beautiful Manifold Valley on your right and a shapely peak, Bunster Hill, on your left. A path takes you across the shoulder of the hill, across the ridge and furrow of a medieval field system, then back into the valley of the Dove.

walk directions

1 Turn right out of the car park and follow the road along the west bank of the Dove. Cross the footbridge to the opposite bank and turn left along a wide footpath. This twists and turns through the narrow dale, between Bunster Hill and Thorpe Cloud.

2 Follow the path as it climbs some steps up through the woods on to the famous rocky outcrop of Lovers' Leap, then descends past the magnificent Tissington Spires and Reynard's Cave. Here a huge natural arch surrounds the much smaller entrance to the historic cave. As the dale narrows the path climbs above the river.

3 The dale widens again. Leave the main path for a route signposted 'Public Footpath to Stanshope', and cross the footbridge over the Dove. A narrow woodland path turns right beneath the huge spire of Ilam Rock above you. Ignore the path on the left, signposted to Ilam '(steep ascent)'. Beyond a stile the path eases to the left into Hall Dale. Following the valley bottom, as it climbs out of the woods into a rugged limestone-cragged gorge.

4 As the gorge begins to become shallow the path enters pastureland – the attractive village of Stanshope is now on the skyline. At a crossroads of paths turn left through a squeeze stile in the wall and head south with a stone wall on the right. Where the wall turns right, keep walking straight ahead to reach another stile, and then veer half right by a wall in the next field. The path cuts diagonally to the left across the last two fields to reach Ilam-Moor Lane, 250yds (229m) to the south of Damgate Farm.

5 Turn left to walk along the lovely quiet country lane. There are magnificent views from here down to Ilam and the Manifold Valley ahead of you and down to the right.

6 After 800yds (732m) take a footpath on the left, following the drive to Ilamtops Farm for a few paces before turning right over a stile. A field path now heads roughly south-east, traversing low grassy fellsides to the top of Moor Plantation woods.

7 Here the path (fallen away in places) cuts across the steep sides of Bunster Hill, before straddling its south spur and descending to a step-stile in the intake wall. A clear path now descends south-east across sloping pastures to the back of the Izaak Walton Hotel.

8 Turn left (north-east) by the hotel across more fields and back to the car park.

Extending the walk

As so often when walking beside the River Dove, it's difficult to resist the temptation to carry on following its lovely series of dales. You can do this at Point A (see map), continuing up the dale to Viator's Bridge, a packhorse bridge in lovely Mill Dale, before heading back across the fields to rejoin the main route at Point B. The bridge on the route takes its name from a character in Izaak Walton's *Compleat Angler*, who complains to his companion Piscator that the bridge is too small – 'Why a mouse can hardly go over it: Tis not two fingers broad.'

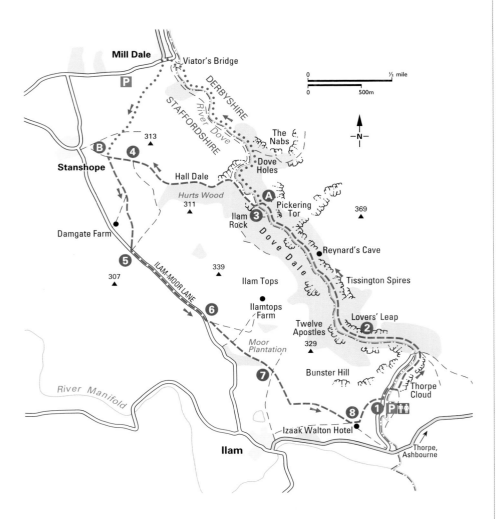

walk information	
► **DISTANCE**	5 miles (8km)
► **MINIMUM TIME**	3hrs 30min
► **ASCENT/GRADIENT**	557ft (170m) ▲▲▲
► **LEVEL OF DIFFICULTY**	🏃🏃🏃
► **PATHS**	Mostly good paths, lanes, a few stiles, one small scramble
► **LANDSCAPE**	Partially wooded dales and high pastures
► **SUGGESTED MAPS**	OS Explorer OL24 White Peak
► **START/FINISH**	Grid reference: SK 146509
► **DOG FRIENDLINESS**	Dogs should be kept under close control
► **PARKING**	Dovedale pay car park, near Thorpe
► **PUBLIC TOILETS**	At car park

A steady climb raises you above the hurly-burly of Matlock Bath to a more familiar Peakland landscape.

Scaling the Heights of Abraham

Between Matlock and Cromford the River Derwent forges its way through a spectacular, thickly wooded limestone gorge. At Matlock Bath it jostles for space with the bustling A6 highway, the railway to Derby and a string of three-storey houses, shops and amusement parlours, built by the Victorians, who flocked here to take in the healing spa waters. On the hillside to the east lies the gaunt castle of Riber, while Alpine-type cable cars glide up the Heights of Abraham, above cliff tops to the west.

ABOVE: Waterfall near Cromford, Derbyshire on the River Derwent in the Peak District
RIGHT: Cable cars sail over the Heights of Abraham; the route is 619yds (568m) long and climbs 554ft (169m)

The Heights in Quebec

The original Heights of Abraham, which the hillside must have resembled, rise above Quebec and the St Lawrence River in Canada. There, in 1759, British troops under General Wolfe fought a victorious battle with the French under General Montcalm. Both generals were killed and the encounter earned Wolfe, and Quebec, an unenviable place in English place-name folklore, to be joined later by Waterloo and later still, Spion Kop.

Matlock Bath

Matlock Bath doesn't have time to catch its breath: it's Derbyshire's mini-Blackpool. Yet there are peaceful corners, and this fine walk seeks them out. It offers good views across the Matlock Gorge. Spurning the cable car, it climbs through the woods and out on to the hillside above the town. The Victoria Prospect Tower peeps over the trees. Built by unemployed miners a century ago it's now part of the Heights of Abraham complex.

Above the complex, a little path leads you through delectable woodland. In spring it's heavy with the scent of wild garlic and coloured by a carpet of bluebells. Out of the woods, an attractive hedge-lined unsurfaced lane weaves its way through high pastures, giving distant views of the White Peak plateau, Black Rocks and the cliffs of Crich Stand.

Bonsall

At the end of the lane, there's Bonsall, whose Perpendicular church tower and spire has been beckoning you onwards for some time. In the centre of this old lead mining village is a sloping market square with a 17th-century cross. The Kings Head Inn, built in 1677, overlooks the square, and is said to be haunted.

The lane out of Bonsall takes you to the edge of an area of old mine shafts and modern-day quarries. Here you're diverted into the woods above the Via Gellia, a valley named after Philip Gell who built the road from the quarry to the Cromford Canal.

Those who wish can make a short diversion from the woodland path to see the Arkwright Centre and the canal in Cromford. The main route swings north, back into the woods of the Derwent Valley, passing the high hamlet of Upperwood, where fleeting views of Matlock appear through the trees.

walk directions

1 Cross the A6 and then take St John's Road up the wooded slopes opposite. It passes beneath St John's Chapel to reach the gates of Cliffe House. Take the path on the right signposted 'Heights of Abraham'. The path climbs steeply upwards through the woods before veering left across the fields above Masson Farm.

2 Beyond the farmhouse and with Victoria Prospect Tower directly ahead, the waymarked path swings right and climbs up to the top of the field. Beyond this the footpath threads through hawthorn thickets before passing one of the entrances to the Heights of Abraham complex.

3 Ignore an obvious, engineered path and continue uphill along the perimeter of the complex and then turn left, going over a wall stile. After crossing a wide vehicle track the narrow footpath re-enters woodland.

4 At the far side of the woods, turn right on to a farm track close to Ember Farm. Join a pleasant lane that winds down pastured hillslopes into Bonsall village.

5 Turn left by the church along a lane that becomes unsurfaced when you get beyond Town End Farm. The lane finally comes to an abrupt end by the high fences of a quarry. Turn left here and follow a wide track around the perimeter of the quarry.

6 Where the fence ends, continue down the track, bending sharply right then left along a narrow path through woodland high above the Via Gellia, then take the left fork after about 300 yds (274m).

7 Turn left when you reach the next junction, following the footpath waymarked for the Derwent Valley Walk (DVW). This climbs further up the wooded bank, then turns left, tracing a mossy wall on the right. It rakes across the wooded hillside, passes above Cromford Court, then climbs away past some cave entrances to a lane at Upperwood. Ignore the next DVW sign and continue along the lane between cottages and past the West Lodge entrance to the Heights of Abraham show caves.

8 After 100yds (91m) leave the surfaced road for a stepped path through the woods on the left, signed 'Matlock'. Climb some steps to a high wooden footbridge over the Heights of Abraham approach road, and then continue on the woodland path. You'll pass under the Heights of Abraham cable cars before joining a farm track that has come in from the left.

9 This joins St John's Lane and the outward route at Cliffe House. Retrace your steps to the start.

walk information

➤ **DISTANCE**	8 miles (12.9km)
➤ **MINIMUM TIME**	4hrs 30min
➤ **ASCENT/GRADIENT**	1,200ft (365m) ▲▲▲
➤ **LEVEL OF DIFFICULTY**	🚶🚶🚶
➤ **PATHS**	Narrow woodland paths, field paths and unsurfaced lanes, lots of stiles
➤ **LANDSCAPE**	Fields and wooded hillsides
➤ **SUGGESTED MAPS**	OS Explorer OL24 White Peak
➤ **START/FINISH**	Grid reference: SK 297595
➤ **DOG FRIENDLINESS**	Dogs on lead over farmland
➤ **PARKING**	Pay car park at Artists Corner
➤ **PUBLIC TOILETS**	At car park

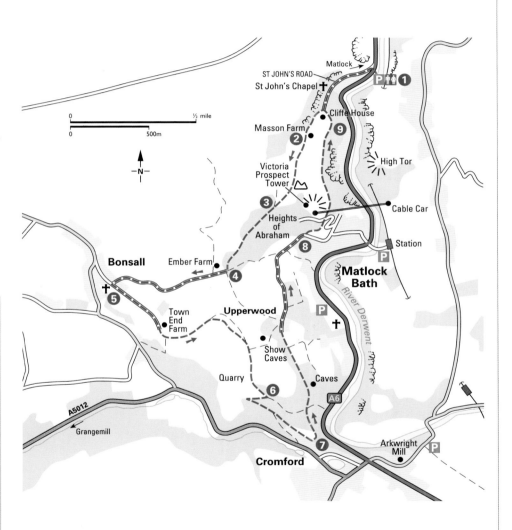

From the coast's wide-open magnificence to a peaceful nature reserve.

A Saint's Tale in Old Hunstanton

ABOVE: The present lighthouse on the cliffs at Hunstanton was built in 1844
LEFT: The eroding cliffs at Hunstanton

Old Hunstanton is steeped in history and legend. It is said that St Edmund was shipwrecked here in AD 855, and was so grateful for being spared a watery death in the Wash that he built a chapel as an act of thanksgiving. The 13th-century ruins still stand today, looking out across grey stormy seas from near the old lighthouse. Edmund left Hunstanton soon after and went on to become King of the East Angles. Between AD 869 and 870 Vikings invaded his kingdom and fought battles until he was captured.

The Miracle of St Edmund

Some years after refusing to renounce his faith and suffering a particularly unpleasant death, Edmund's grave was dug up and his body was found to be uncorrupted. It was declared a miracle and his remains were moved around the country for many years in an attempt to keep them safe from Vikings. They were eventually kept in Bury St Edmunds, although records are vague about what happened to them later. Some say they were taken to France, while others claim he was reinterred at Bury after the Reformation. Regardless of the fate of the relics, Hunstanton is still proud of its claim to a small piece of the saint's history.

Antics in the Wash

Edmund is not the only remarkable historical figure to be associated with the village. Members of the Le Strange family have been squires and landlords here for more than 800 years. They laid claim to the beach and, according to one charter, all that is in the sea for as far as a horseman can hurl a spear at low tide. The family still holds the title of Lord High Admiral of the Wash. There is a popular local story that tells of a famous German lady swimmer called Mercedes Gleitze performing the impressive feat of swimming the Wash from Lincolnshire to Norfolk in the 1930s and the admiral promptly stepping forward to claim her as his rightful property!

Listening Posts and Smugglers' Tales

The lighthouse that has become a symbol of this attractive town dates from 1830. When the First World War broke out in 1914, the light was extinguished and was never lit again. The lighthouse is now in private hands. Because of its strategic position on the coast, Hunstanton was the site of some very clandestine happenings in that war. Hippesley Hut, a bungalow, was used to house a secret listening post to monitor the activities of German Zeppelins and some of its secrets remain hidden even today.

Before you leave the village, spare a thought for poor William Green, a Light Dragoon officer, who was shot here in 1784 by smugglers while helping the King's customs men. The killers were never brought to justice, although the villagers, being such a small community, must have known their identities. The association of the village with contraband can be seen in the name Smugglers' Lane, along which you will walk.

walk directions

1 Walk towards the sea and turn left to head across the dunes. This is Norfolk at its best, with miles of sandy beaches and dunes, and the lighthouse at Old Hunstanton visible on a cliff. Keep close to the golf course and after about a mile (1.6km) you will arrive at a colourful row of beach huts.

2 When you see a gap in the fence to your left, take the path across the golf course and continue straight ahead into Smugglers' Lane. Emerging at a junction, take the lane opposite, past the post box to reach Caley Hall Hotel. Cross the A149 and aim for the road signed 'To St Mary's Church', where you can see the grave of William Green.

3 Turn right up Chapel Bank, through a tunnel of shade before reaching open farmland. After 700yds (640m), turn left on a grassy track, Lovers Lane, a permissive path. When you reach Lodge Farm, follow the track around farm buildings to a lane.

4 Turn left along the route marked Norfolk County Council Ringstead Rides. When you see the fairy-tale lodge of Hunstanton Park ahead, follow the lane round to the right along an avenue of mature trees. In the field to your right you will see the ruins of 13th-century St Andrew's Chapel.

5 Bear left at Downs Farm and head for the gate to enter Ringstead Downs Nature Reserve, one of just a few areas in Norfolk that is chalk rather than sand. It belongs to the Norfolk Wildlife Trust and the area

walk information

➤ DISTANCE	8 miles (12.9km)
➤ MINIMUM TIME	3hrs 30min
➤ ASCENT/GRADIENT	164ft (50m) ▲▲▲
➤ LEVEL OF DIFFICULTY	🚶🚶🚶
➤ PATHS	Country tracks, lanes, muddy paths and sand dunes, 1 stile
➤ LANDSCAPE	Sandy beaches, rolling chalk valleys and farmland
➤ SUGGESTED MAPS	OS Explorer 250 Norfolk Coast West
➤ START/FINISH	Grid reference: TF 697438
➤ DOG FRIENDLINESS	On lead in nature reserves and on farmland
➤ PARKING	Beach car park at Holme next the Sea (pay at kiosk)
➤ PUBLIC TOILETS	By beach car park

is grazed by traditional hill sheep. This is one of the most beautiful parts of the walk. Follow the path right through the reserve until you reach a lane.

6 Turn left into Ringstead, where the tower of St Peter's Church still stands. Stay on this road as it bends right and left through the village, passing The Gin Trap Inn. The road climbs gently out of the village, forking right then left along Peddars Way towards a sail-less windmill.

7 At the last house, look for the waymarked path to the left. This cuts across a field, then turns right into a lovely tunnel of hedges. Note the Norfolk Songline sculpture half-way along the path.

8 Cross the A149 and walk through Holme village, with its long green to reach the car park.

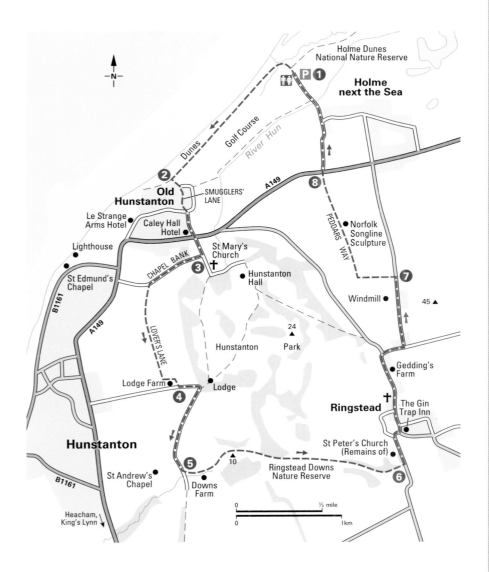

Walk along the sea defences to some of the finest bird reserves in the country.

Blakeney Eye's Magical Marshes

ABOVE: A windmill stands on the riverbank at Cley next the Sea
LEFT: Fishing boats moored in Blakeney harbour

Blakeney was a prosperous port in medieval times, but went into decline when its sea channels began to silt up. However, although the merchants decried the slow accumulation of salt marsh and sand bars, birds began to flock here in their thousands. By Victorian times it had become a favoured spot for shooting. Some sportsmen just wanted to kill the many waterfowl, while others were more interested in trophy collecting — looking for species that were rare or little-known. Many of these hapless birds ended up stuffed and in museums or private collections.

Nature Reserve

After many years of bird shooting by visiting sportsmen, the National Trust arrived in 1912 and purchased the area from Cley Beach to the tip of the sand and shingle peninsula of Blakeney Point. It became one of the first nature reserves to be safeguarded in Britain. Today it is a fabulous place for a walk, regardless of whether you are interested in ornithology. A bright summer day will show you glittering streams, salt-scented grasses waving gently in the breeze and pretty-sailed yachts bobbing in the distance. By contrast, a wet and windy day in winter will reveal the stark beauty of this place, with the distant roar of white-capped waves pounding the beach, rain-drenched vegetation and a menacing low-hung sky filled with scudding clouds. Whatever the weather, a walk at Blakeney is always invigorating.

Although these days we regard the Victorians' wholesale slaughter of wildlife with distaste, they did leave a legacy of valuable information. It was 19th-century trophy hunters who saw the Pallas' warbler and the yellow-breasted bunting in Britain for the first time – and they were seen at Blakeney. A little later, when the Cley Bird Observatory operated here between 1949 and 1963, the first subalpine warbler in Norfolk was captured and ringed.

The Victorians' records tell us that a good many red-spotted bluethroats appeared in September and October, and any collector who happened to visit then was almost certain to bag one. In the 1950s the observatory discovered that these were becoming rare at this time of year. Today, bluethroats are regular spring visitors but are seldom seen in the autumn. It is thought that this change over time is related to different weather patterns and indicates how climate change, even on this small scale, can dramatically affect the behaviour of birds.

RIGHT: The harbour and the surrounding marshes at Blakeney are owned by the National Trust

RIGHT: Pretty flowers in a garden at Blakeney
ABOVE: The village sign at Blakeney displays a seafaring history as well as the wildlife of the local area

walk directions

1 From the car park head for the wildfowl conservation project, a fenced-off area teeming with ducks, geese and widgeon. A species list has been mounted on one side, so you can see how many you can spot. Take the path marked Norfolk Coast Path out towards the marshes. This raised bank is part of the sea defences, and is managed by the Environment Agency. Eventually, you have salt marshes on both sides.

2 At the turning, head east. Carmelite friars once lived around here, although there is little to see of their chapel, the remains of which are located just after you turn by the wooden staithe (landing stage) to head south again. This part of the walk is excellent for spotting kittiwakes and terns in late summer. Also, look for Sabine's gull, manx and sooty shearwaters, godwits, turnstones and curlews. The path leads you past Cley Windmill, built in 1810 and which last operated in 1919. It is open to visitors and you can climb to the top to enjoy the view across the marshes. Follow signs for the Norfolk Coast Path until you reach the A149.

3 Cross the A149 to the pavement opposite, then turn right. Take the first left after crossing the little creek. Eventually you reach the cobblestone houses of Wiveton and a crossroads; go straight ahead.

4 Take the grassy track opposite Primrose Farm, to a T-junction. This is Blakeney Road; turn right along it. However, if you want refreshments before the homeward stretch, turn left and walk a short way to the Wiveton Bell. The lane is wide and ahead you will see St Nicholas' Church nestling among trees. This dates from the 13th century, but was extended in the 14th. Its two towers served as navigation beacons for sailors, and the east, narrower one is floodlit at night.

5 At the A149 there are two lanes opposite you. Take the High Street fork on the left to walk through the centre of Blakeney village. Many cottages are owned by the Blakeney Neighbourhood Housing Society, which rents homes to those locals unable to buy their own. Don't miss the 14th-century Guildhall undercroft at the bottom of Mariner's Hill. After you have explored the area, continue to the car park.

walk information

➤ **DISTANCE**	4.5 miles (7.2km)
➤ **MINIMUM TIME**	2hrs
➤ **ASCENT/GRADIENT**	98ft (30m)
➤ **LEVEL OF DIFFICULTY**	
➤ **PATHS**	Footpaths with some paved lanes, can flood in winter
➤ **LANDSCAPE**	Salt marshes, scrubby meadows and farmland
➤ **SUGGESTED MAPS**	OS Explorer 251 Norfolk Coast Central
➤ **START/FINISH**	Grid reference: TG 028442
➤ **DOG FRIENDLINESS**	Under control as these are important refuges for birds
➤ **PARKING**	Carnser (pay) car park, on seafront opposite Blakeney Guildhall and Manor Hotel
➤ **PUBLIC TOILETS**	Across road from Carnser car park

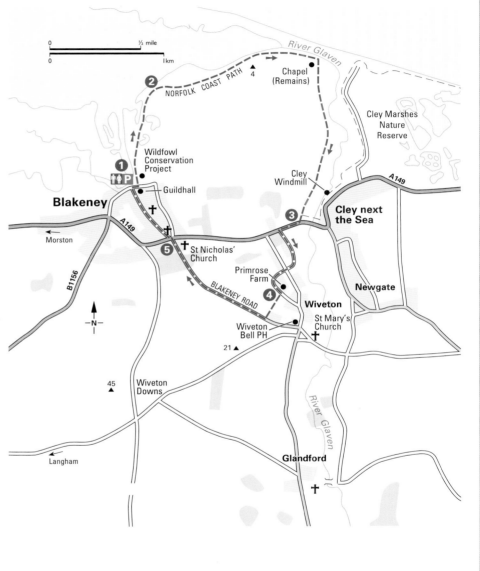

Through the wooded By Brook Valley from a famous picture-book village.

Castle Combe and By Brook

Since being voted 'the prettiest village in England' in 1962, there have been more visitors to Castle Combe, more photographs taken of it and more words written about it than any other village in the county. Nestling deep in a stream-threaded combe, just a mile (1.6km), and a world away, from the M4, it certainly has all the elements to make it a tourist's dream. By Brook is the name of the pretty little river that trickles through it.

ABOVE: An attractive cottage in Water Lane, Castle Combe
LEFT: Ivy-clad cottages in the village

Royal Assent

Dover's Hill is named after the founder of the Cotswold Olimpicks, Robert Dover. Established with the permission of James I, they were dubbed 'royal' games, and indeed have taken place during the reigns of 14 monarchs. Dover was born in Norfolk in 1582. He was educated at Cambridge and then was called to the bar. His profession brought him to the Cotswolds but he had memories of the plays and spectacles that he had seen in the capital.

The Main Event

It is accepted that the first games took place in 1612, but they may well have begun at an earlier date. It is also possible that Dover was simply reviving an existing ancient festivity. Initially, at least, the main events were horse-racing and hare-coursing, the prizes being, respectively, a silver castle ornament and a silver-studded collar. Other competitions in these early games were for running, jumping, throwing, wrestling and staff fighting. The area was festooned with yellow flags and ribbons and there were dancing events as well as pavilions for chess and other cerebral contests.

Annual Event

The Olimpicks soon became an indispensable part of the local Whitsuntide festivities, with mention of them even being made in Shakespeare's work. Robert Dover managed the games for 30 years and he died in 1652. The games continued in a variety of forms throughout the following centuries, surviving several attempts to suppress them when

LEFT: Main Street, Chipping Campden
RIGHT: Distant view across fields of the village of Chipping Campden in the evening
PAGE 71: Chipping Campden Church from the south-east

they became more rowdy and seemed to present a threat to public order and safety. They finally became an established annual event once again in 1966.

Nowadays, the games are more like a cross between pantomime and carnival, but they have retained their atmosphere of local showmanship. At the end of the evening's events all the spectators, holding flaming torches, file down the road back into Chipping Campden, where the festivities continue with dancing and music along the main street and in the square.

The Wool Town

It's worth lingering in Chipping Campden, before or after the walk. Possibly the most beautiful of all the Cotswold towns, it was once famous throughout Europe as the centre of the English wool trade. A leisurely stroll along its curving High Street of handsome stone houses is a must. The church, too, is particularly fine and it's also worthwhile searching out the Ernest Wilson Memorial Garden, on the High Street.

walk information

➤ **DISTANCE**	5 miles (8km)
➤ **MINIMUM TIME**	2hrs
➤ **ASCENT/GRADIENT**	280ft (85m) ▲▲▲
➤ **LEVEL OF DIFFICULTY**	🚶🚶🚶
➤ **PATHS**	Fields, roads and tracks, 8 stiles
➤ **LANDSCAPE**	Open hillside, woodland and village
➤ **SUGGESTED MAPS**	OS Explorer OL45 The Cotswolds
➤ **START/FINISH**	Grid reference: SP 151391
➤ **DOG FRIENDLINESS**	Suitable in parts (particularly Dover's Hill) but livestock in some fields
➤ **PARKING**	Chipping Campden High Street or main square
➤ **PUBLIC TOILETS**	A short way down Sheep Street

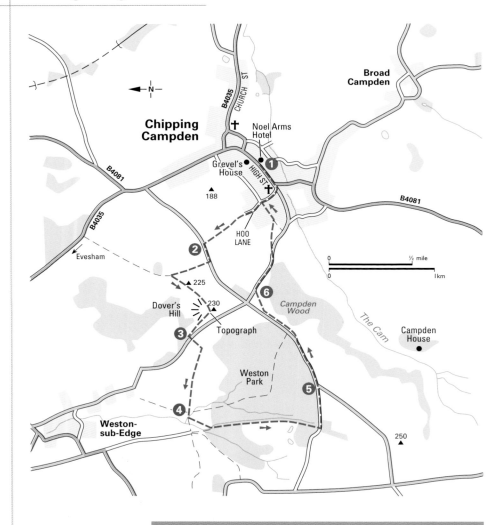

Chipping Campden

Broad Campden

Noel Arms Hotel

Grevel's House

Evesham

HOO LANE

Dover's Hill

Topograph

Campden Wood

The Cam

Campden House

Weston Park

Weston-sub-Edge

½ mile

1km

walk directions

1   Turn left from the Noel Arms, continue to the Catholic church, and turn right into West End Terrace. Where this bears right, go straight ahead on Hoo Lane. Follow this up to a right turn, with farm buildings on your left. Continue uphill to a path and keep going to a road.

2   Turn left for around 100 paces and then right to cross to a path. Follow this between hedges to a kissing gate. Through this turn left on to Dover's Hill, with extensive views before you, and walk along the escarpment edge, which drops away to your right. Pass a trig point and then a topograph. Now go right, down the slope, to a second kissing gate on the left.

3   Cross the road to a stile into a field. Cross this to a stile, then to a kissing gate by a horse shelter, then head to a gate in the bottom right-hand corner. Head straight down the next field. At a double stile go into another field and, keeping to the left of a fence, continue to another stile. Head down the next field, cross a track and then find adjacent stiles in the bottom left corner.

4   Cross the first one and walk along the bottom of a field. Keep the stream and fence to your right and look for a double stile and footbridge in the far corner. Go over, crossing the stream, and then turn left, following a rising woodland path alongside the stream. Enter a field through a gate and continue ahead to meet a track. Stay on this track, passing through gateposts and over a stile, until you come to a country lane and turn left.

5   After 400yds (366m) reach a busier road and turn left for a further 450yds (411m). Shortly before the road curves left, drop to the right on to a field path parallel with the road. About 200yds (183m) before the next corner go half right down the field to a road.

6   Turn right, down the road. Shortly after a cottage on the right, go left into a field. Turn right over a stile and go half left to the corner. Pass through a kissing gate, cross a road among houses and continue into Birdcage Walk, then turn right to return to the centre of Chipping Campden.

A stroll through the countryside around Slad, backcloth to Laurie Lee's most popular novel.

Walking with Rosie in the Slad Valley

The Slad Valley is one of the least spoiled parts of the Cotswolds, which is surprising considering its long-standing and well-known association with the area's most important literary figure, the poet Laurie Lee (1914–97). Lee's grave can be found in the churchyard here at Slad. Lee is not instantly remembered for his poetry but for *Cider With Rosie* (1959), his autobiographical account of a Cotswold childhood. The novel has, for thousands of schoolchildren, been part of their English Literature syllabus.

ABOVE: Laurie Lee's gravestone at Slad
RIGHT: The River Colne meanders through tranquil meadows at Cassey Compton

A Childhood Gone Forever

For anyone coming to the area, *Cider With Rosie* is well worth reading. It is largely set in Slad, where Lee was brought up and lived for much of his life. The book charts, in poetic language, the experiences of a child living in a world that is within living memory and yet has quite disappeared. Some of the episodes recounted in the book are said to have been products of Lee's imagination but, as he said himself, it was the 'feeling' of his childhood that he was endeavouring to capture.

A Spanish Odyssey

The story of his life is, anyway, an interesting one. He spent a considerable time in Spain and became involved in the Spanish Civil War and the struggle against Franco. Afterwards he established a reputation as a poet, mixing with the literati of the day. He was never very prolific – much of his energy appears to have been poured into love affairs. He did, however, write plays for radio and was involved in film-making during World War II. But it was with the publication of *Cider With Rosie* that he became a household name. Readers from all over the world identified with his magical evocation of rural English life and the book has not been out of print since. To some extent Lee became a prisoner of a *Cider With Rosie* industry. The picture of an avuncular figure living a bucolic idyll was not a strictly accurate one – much of his time was spent in London. He was susceptible to illness all his life. Nonetheless, in his later years he managed to complete his autobiographical trilogy. His second volume, *As I Walked Out One Midsummer Morning* (1969) describes his journey from Gloucestershire to Spain as an itinerant fiddle player. The third, *A Moment of War* (1991), recounts his experiences there during the Civil War. Lee died in 1997 and is buried in Slad churchyard. Many of the places in and around the village mentioned in *Cider With Rosie* are readily identifiable today. Although it is no longer possible to frolic in the roads with impunity, the valley remains as beautiful as it ever was.

RIGHT: The River Coln flowing through the narrow Cotswold valley of Slad at Coln St Dennis

walk information

➤ **DISTANCE**	3.75 miles (6km)
➤ **MINIMUM TIME**	2hrs
➤ **ASCENT/GRADIENT**	425ft (130m) ▲▲△
➤ **LEVEL OF DIFFICULTY**	🜂🜂🜂
➤ **PATHS**	Tracks, fields and quiet lanes, 17 stiles
➤ **LANDSCAPE**	Hills, valleys and woodland
➤ **SUGGESTED MAPS**	OS Explorer 179 Gloucester, Cheltenham & Stroud
➤ **START/FINISH**	Grid reference: SO 878087
➤ **DOG FRIENDLINESS**	Mostly off lead – livestock encountered occasionally
➤ **PARKING**	Lay-by at Bull's Cross
➤ **PUBLIC TOILETS**	None en route

walk directions

1 From Bull's Cross walk to the south end of the lay-by and turn left on to a tarmac-covered footpath, the Wysis Way. Follow it down and, immediately before Trillgate Farm, turn left over a stile into a field. Go half right, down the field and up the other side, to a gate and stile at the top. Turn left along a track. Where it joins another track stay right and continue to a lane.

2 Turn right and walk to the bottom. Pass Steanbridge Mill and if you want to visit Slad, follow the lane into the village. To continue the walk turn left immediately after the large pond along a restricted byway and walk to a stile. Cross into a field, with a hedge on your right, and continue to a stile at the top.

3 Cross and follow a path to another stile. Follow the left side of the next field and go over another stile, then continue along the path. Pass through a gate on to a track, stay to the right of Furners Farm and curve left. About 30yds (27m) after the curve turn right over a stile on to a wooded path and after 130yds (118m) go right again over a stile into a field. Walk ahead, with the farm above you and to the right. Cross another stile and then keep to the right of a small pond.

4 At the top of the pond cross a stile into a field. Go half left across it to a gate and stile. In the next field head straight across its lower part. At a point where a telegraph pole stands close to a hedge, turn right over a stile on to a track. Turn left to meet a lane.

5 Turn right and follow the lane to the valley bottom. Start to climb the other side and at a corner go over a stile on your right by The Vatch Cottage. Ascend steeply, skirting the garden, to another stile at the road. Turn right along the pavement. After 150yds (137m) bear left on to a public

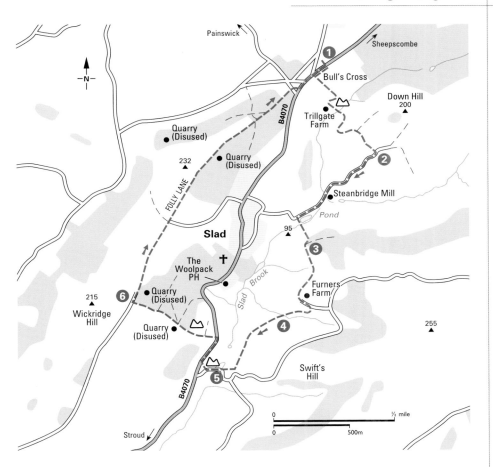

footpath and climb steeply. At a junction of footpaths bear left and continue to a field. Follow the margin of the field up to a stile, then follow the path as it weaves between a dry-stone wall and the edge of woodland.

6 At the top go over a stile, turn right on to Folly Lane and continue to a junction. If you want to go into Slad, turn right, otherwise continue ahead on to a path that will soon take you through the Frith Wood Nature Reserve. Walk through the woods, finally emerging at your starting point at Bull's Cross.

Discovering three of Gloucestershire's finest villages, which were saved from decline and decay.

Stanton and Stanway from Snowshill

Villages in the Cotswolds have not always been prosperous. Many, like Stanton and Snowshill, were owned by great abbeys, but they passed to private landlords after the Dissolution of the Monasteries. Subsistence farmers were edged out by short leases and enclosure of fields. Villagers who had farmed their own strips of land became labourers. The number of small farmers decreased dramatically and, with the onset of the Industrial Revolution, so too did the demand for labour. Cheaper food flooded in from overseas and catastrophic harvests compounded the problem.

ABOVE: Summer sunshine filters through the trees at Cranham Woods
RIGHT: Stone-built cottages line the streets of Stanton, which was restored in the 20th century by Sir Philip Stott

To the Cities

People left the countryside in droves to work in the industrial towns and cities. Cotswold villages, once at the core of the most important woollen industry in medieval Europe, gradually became impoverished backwaters. But the structures themselves resisted decay. Unlike villages in many other parts of Britain, their buildings were made of stone. Enlightened landlords, who cherished their innate beauty, turned them into restoration projects.

Enlightened Landlords

The three villages encountered on this walk are living reminders of this process. Snowshill, together with Stanton, was once owned by Winchcombe Abbey. In 1539 it became the property of Henry VIII's sixth wife, Catherine Parr. The manor house was transformed into the estate's administrative centre and remained in the Parr family until 1919. Then the estate was bought by Charles Wade, a sugar plantation owner. He restored the house and devoted his time to amassing an extraordinary collection of art and artefacts, which he subsequently bequeathed to the National Trust. Now forming the basis of a museum, his collection, from Japanese armour to farm machinery, is of enormous appeal. Next on this walk comes Stanway, a small hamlet at the centre of a large estate owned by Lord Neidpath. The most striking feature here is the magnificent gatehouse to the Jacobean Stanway House, a gem of Cotswold architecture built around 1630.

Restored Houses

The village of Stanton comes last on this walk. It was rescued from decay and oblivion in 1906 by the architect Sir Philip Stott. He bought and restored Stanton Court and many of the village's 16th-century houses. The peaceful parish church is located along a lane leading from the market cross. It has two pulpits (one dating from the 14th century, the other Jacobean) and a west gallery added by the Victorian restorer Sir Ninian Comper.

➤ **DISTANCE**	7 miles (11.3km)
➤ **MINIMUM TIME**	2hrs 45min
➤ **ASCENT/GRADIENT**	625ft (190m) ▲▲▲
➤ **LEVEL OF DIFFICULTY**	♦♦♦♦
➤ **PATHS**	Tracks, estate grassland and pavement, 1 stile
➤ **LANDSCAPE**	High grassland, open wold, wide-ranging views and villages
➤ **SUGGESTED MAPS**	OS Explorer OL45 The Cotswolds
➤ **START/FINISH**	Grid reference: SP 096341
➤ **DOG FRIENDLINESS**	On lead – livestock on most parts of walk
➤ **PARKING**	Snowshill village (free car park to north of the village)
➤ **PUBLIC TOILETS**	None en route

ABOVE: *Detail on the gatehouse at Stanway House*
LEFT: *Hilly and wooded landscape near Stanton*
PAGE 81: *Gravestones at Snowshill village*

walk directions

1   From the free car park walk into Snowshill village, descending to the right at a Y-junction past Snowshill Manor and the church on your left. After a 0.25-mile (400m) climb turn right down a lane signed 'Sheepscombe House'. After another 0.25 mile (400m), at a right-hand bend on the crest of the hill, turn left up to a gate and enter a field.

2   Go half right to a gate. In the next field go half right to the far corner and left along a track. Take the second footpath on the right through a gate into a field and walk half left to another gate. Cross straight ahead through the field to another gate on to a track.

3   Ignoring the footpath to your right, walk down a stony track with a wood on your right. After 275yds (251m) turn right on to a stony track, veering right just before a stone barn. The track descends steeply through Lidcombe Wood. After 0.5 mile (800m), where it flattens out, a farm comes into view across fields to the right, after which the track bears left uphill. Continue straight along the track, which becomes a narrow footpath, to a road.

4   Walk along the pavement and, after 500yds (457m), turn right through a gate into a small orchard. Walk half left across this, bearing slightly right, to arrive at a kissing gate. Go through this and walk with a high wall to your right, to reach a road.

5   Turn right and pass the impressive entrance to Stanway House and Stanway church, both on your right. Follow the road as it goes right. Shortly after another entrance turn right through a gate opposite a thatched cricket pavilion. Go half left to another stile and in the next large field go half right.

6   Now walk all the way into Stanton, following the regular and clear waymarkers of the Cotswold Way. After 1 mile (1.6km) you will arrive at a gate at the edge of Stanton. Turn left along a lane to a junction. Turn right here and walk through the village, turning right at the war memorial. Where the road goes left, walk straight on, passing the stone cross and then another footpath. Climb up to pass to the right of the

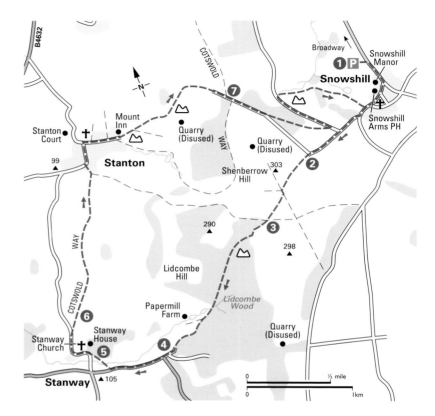

Mount Inn. Beyond it walk up a steep, shaded path to a gate. Then walk straight up the hill on a stony track (ignoring a path to the right after a few paces). Climb all the way to the top to meet a lane, passing through two gates.

7   Ignore the 'Cotswold Way' sign and walk down the lane for 250yds (229m) then turn left through a kissing gate into woodland. Follow the path, going left at a fork. At the bottom cross a stile, continuing in the field to a kissing gate in the far corner by the road. Pass through and turn left and walk for 600yds (549m). Before a cottage turn right through a gate into a scrubby field. Descend steeply to the far side and turn right through a gate. Continue to a stile on your right, cross it and turn left. Follow the margin of this grassy area to a track, then a gate, and then follow the path back into Snowshill.

An exhilarating walk on a spectacular piece of coastline.

Lulworth to Durdle Door

L ulworth Cove is an almost perfectly circular bay in the rolling line of cliffs that form Dorset's southern coast. It earned World Heritage status in 2002. The cove provides a secure anchorage for small fishing boats and pleasure craft, and a sun-trap of safe water for summer bathers. The cliffs around the eastern side of the bay are crumbly soft and brightly coloured in some places, while around the opposite arm the rock appears to have been folded and shoved aside by an unseen hand. The geology is intriguing and a visit to the Heritage Centre will help you to sort it out.

ABOVE: *Fossil Forest at Lulworth Cove, Dorset*
RIGHT: *Boats in front of the hills at West Lulworth*

Lulworth's Geology

The oldest layer, easily identified here, is the gleaming white Portland stone. This attractive stone was much employed by Christopher Wren in his rebuilding of London. It is a fine-grained oolite, around 140 million years old. It consists of tightly compressed, fossilised shells – the flat-coiled ones are ammonites. Occasional giant ammonites, called titanites, may be seen incorporated into house walls across Purbeck. Like the rock of Bat's Head, it may contain speckled bands of flinty chert. Above this is a layer of Purbeck marble, a limestone rich in the fossils of vertebrates. This is where dinosaur, fish and reptile fossils are usually found. The soft layer above this consists of Wealden beds, a belt of colourful clays, silts and sands, that are unstable and prone to landslips when exposed.

Crumbly, white chalk overlays the Wealden beds. The chalk consists of the remains of microscopic sea creatures and shells deposited over a long period of time when a deep sea covered much of Dorset, some 75 million years ago. This is the chalk that underlies Dorset's famous downland and is seen in the exposed soft, eroded cliffs at White Nothe. Hard nodules and bands of flint appear in the chalk – it's a purer type of chert – and in its gravel beach form it protects long stretches of this fragile coast.

The laying down of chalk marks the end of the Cretaceous period. After this the blanket of chalk was uplifted, folded and subjected to erosion by the slow, inexorable movement of tectonic plates. The Dorset coast was exposed to some of its most extreme pressure between 24 and 1.5 million years ago, resulting in folding, crumpling or overturning of strata. You can see this in the vertical strata on rocks around Durdle Door and Stair Hole.

LEFT & RIGHT: The rocky coastline of Lulworth Cove
NEXT PAGE: Small craft in Lulworth's natural harbour

1 Find the gate at the back of the car park. Pass through this to take the broad, paved footpath that leads up some shallow steps to the top of the first hill. Continue along the brow, and down the other side. Pass below a caravan park and through a gate.

2 Reach the cove of Durdle Door, almost enclosed from the sea by a line of rocks. A flight of steps leads down to the sea here, but carry on walking straight ahead on the coast path and the natural stone arch of the Door itself is revealed in a second cove below you. The mass of Swyre Head looms close and yes, that is the path you're going to take, ascending straight up the side. Walk down to the bottom then climb back up to Swyre Head. The path leads steeply down again on the other side, to a short stretch overlooking Bat's Head. Climb the next steep hill. Continue along the path behind the cliffs, where the land tilts away from the sea.

3 The path climbs more gently up the next hill. Pass a navigation obelisk on the right, and follow the path as it curves round the contour above West Bottom.

4 At a marker stone that indicates Whitenothe ahead turn right, through a gate, and follow a fence inland. The path curves round so you're walking parallel with the coast on level greensward. Pass three stone embrasures with shell sculptures inside, and a second obelisk. Go through a gate. Now keep straight ahead along the top of the field and across a crossing of paths, signed to Daggers Gate. Go through a gateway and straight on. The path starts to descend gently. In the next field the path becomes more of a track. Bear right to pass close by a tumulus and reach a gate.

5 Cross this and walk along the top of the field, above Scratchy Bottom. Cross a stile into a green lane leading to Newlands Farm. Follow it to the right, and turn right into the caravan park. Go straight ahead on the road through here. At the far side go through a gate and turn left, signed to West Lulworth. Stay along the field-edge and walk above a farm lane, around the end of the hill. Keep straight on at the fingerpost and reach the gate above the car park. Turn left and retrace your route.

walk information

➤ DISTANCE	6.75 miles (10.9km)
➤ MINIMUM TIME	3hrs
➤ ASCENT/GRADIENT	1,247ft (380m) ▲▲▲
➤ LEVEL OF DIFFICULTY	🚶🚶🚶🚶
➤ PATHS	Stone path, grassy tracks, tarmac, muddy field path, 4 stiles
➤ LANDSCAPE	Steeply rolling cliffs beside sea, green inland
➤ SUGGESTED MAPS	OS Explorer OL15 Purbeck & South Dorset
➤ START/FINISH	Grid reference: SY 821800
➤ DOG FRIENDLINESS	Excitable dogs need strict control near cliff edge
➤ PARKING	Pay-and-display car park (busy), signed at Lulworth Cove
➤ PUBLIC TOILETS	Beside Heritage Centre; also just above Lulworth Cove

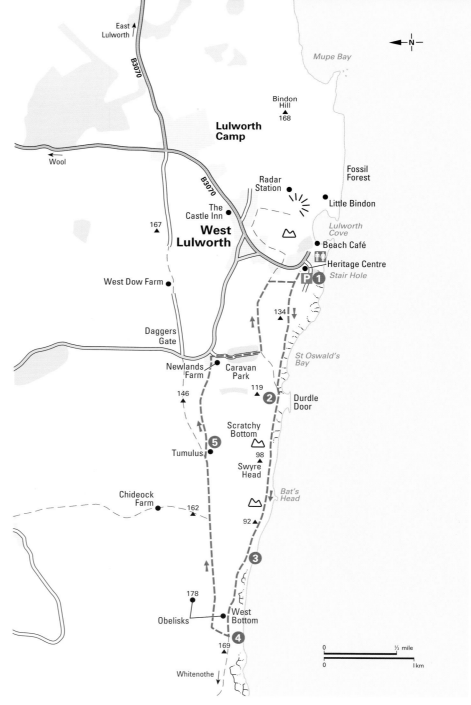

On the trail of Exmoor's red deer in the woodlands under Dunkery Beacon.

Horner's Corners

Horner takes its name from the Saxon 'hwrnwr', a wonderfully expressive word meaning snorer, that here describes the rumble of the stream in its enclosed valley. Above the treetops, Webber's Post is a splendid viewpoint out across the Bristol Channel. What Mr Webber stood there to view, though, was the hunting of red deer.

ABOVE: Walkers among the heather on Exmoor
NEXT PAGE: Valley of the Rocks, Lynton, Exmoor

The Exmoor Stag

The herd on Exmoor numbers several thousand. Although this is small compared to those in the Scottish Highlands, the Exmoor stag himself is the UK's biggest wild deer. This is simply because his life is slightly easier – farmed deer are larger again. On Exmoor, as in the rest of Northern Europe outside Scotland, the deer remains a forest animal. Exmoor's mix of impenetrable woodland with areas of open grazing, even with all its houses, farms and fields, remains good deer country.

The calf is born dappled for camouflage under the trees, and lies in shelter during the day while the hind feeds. If you do come across a deer calf, leave it alone – it hasn't been abandoned. During the summer the stags and hinds run in separate herds. In the Scottish Highlands deer graze on high ground by day to escape from midges, and descend to the forest at night; on Exmoor the main pest is the human, so the deer graze the moor at dawn and dusk, and spend the day in the trees.

Stag Nights

In September and October comes the spectacular rut, when stags roar defiance at each other, and, if that fails, do battle with antlers for mating privileges. During this time they eat only occasionally, fight a lot and mate as often as possible. The stag with a mighty roar and a hard head can gather a harem of a dozen hinds. Your best chance of seeing one is very early or very late in the day – or else in the forest. You may well smell the deer, even though it probably smelled you first and has already gone quietly away. Look closely, too, at the small brown cows two fields away – they may well actually turn out to be deer – binoculars are a must.

While deer are thriving, it is the Exmoor stag hunters that are in danger of extinction. Just one pack of the traditional staghounds remains. The National Trust banned hunting from its land, and the national government has now criminalised it along with fox-hunting.

walk information

➤ **DISTANCE**	4.5 miles (7.2km)
➤ **MINIMUM TIME**	2hrs 30min
➤ **ASCENT/GRADIENT**	1,000ft (305m) ▲▲▲
➤ **LEVEL OF DIFFICULTY**	🚶🚶🚶🚶
➤ **PATHS**	Broad paths, with some stonier ones, steep in places, no stiles
➤ **LANDSCAPE**	Dense woodland in steep-sided stream valleys
➤ **SUGGESTED MAPS**	OS Explorer OL9 Exmoor
➤ **START/FINISH**	Grid reference: SS 898455
➤ **DOG FRIENDLINESS**	Off lead, but be aware of deer and horse-riders
➤ **PARKING**	National Trust car park (free) at Horner
➤ **PUBLIC TOILETS**	At car park

walk directions

1 Leave the National Trust car park in Horner village past the toilets and turn right to the track leading into Horner Wood. This crosses a bridge and passes a field before rejoining Horner Water. You can take a footpath alongside the stream instead of the track, they lead to the same place. Ignore the first footbridge, and continue along the obvious track to where a sign, 'Dunkery Beacon', points to the left towards a second footbridge.

2 Ignore this footbridge as well. Keep on the track for another 100yds (91m), then fork left on a path alongside West Water. This rejoins the track, and after another 0.5mile (800m) alongside the track is another footbridge.

3 Cross to a path that slants up to the right. After 200yds (183m) turn left into a smaller path that turns uphill alongside Prickslade Combe. The path reaches the combe's little stream at a cross-path, with the wood top visible above. Here turn left, across the stream, on a path

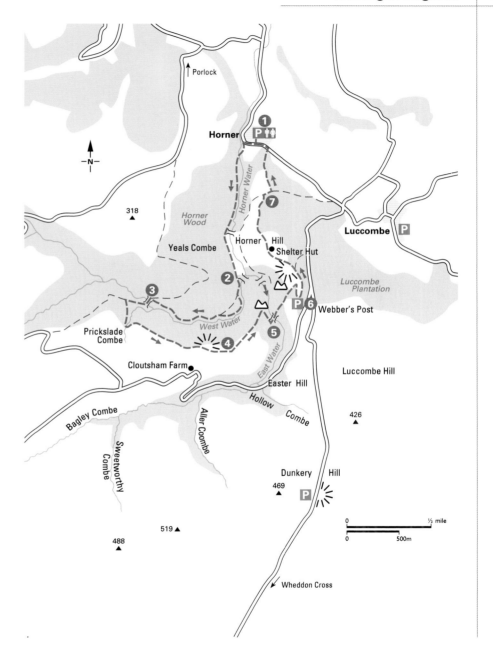

contouring through the top of the wood. After a dip and climb, it emerges into the open and arrives at a fine view over the top of the woodlands to Porlock Bay. It joins a bridleway near a lone pine with a bench.

4 Continue ahead on the bridleway's grassy track, with the car park of Webber's Post visible ahead. Alas, the deep valley of the East Water lies between you and your destination. So, in 55yds (50m), fork down left on a clear path back into birchwoods. This zig-zags down to meet a larger track in the valley bottom.

5 Turn downstream, crossing a footbridge over the East Water, beside a ford. After about 60yds (55m) bear right on to an ascending path. At the top of the steep section turn right on a small sunken path that climbs to the right to Webber's Post car park.

6 Walk to the left, round the car park, to a path to Horner. (Or you could take the pink-surfaced, easy-access path immediately to the right.) The path runs immediately below the 'easy access' one with its stone bench. Just after the concrete sculpture where easy access turns back, bear left on a wider path, soon passing a wooden shelter hut. Again fork left on a wider path to keep ahead down a wide, gentle spur, with the deep valley of the Horner Water on your left. As the spur steepens, the footpath meets a crossing track signposted 'Windsor Path'.

7 Turn right for perhaps 30 paces, then take a descending path signposted 'Horner'. Narrow at first, this widens and finally meets a wide, horse-mangled track with wooden steps; turn left down this into Horner.

RIGHT: A view of Exmoor National Park from Dunkery Beacon

*The River Bovey woodlands and the old
Newton Abbot-to-Moretonhampstead
railway line.*

The Dartmoor National Park Authority at Bovey Tracey

*ABOVE: Traditional thatched cottages at
Buckland in the Moor
LEFT: Dartmoor National Park*

The road signs as you approach Bovey Tracey proudly proclaim the town to be the 'Gateway to the Moor', and although this may be debatable (the town is 3 miles/4.8km from the open moor, and gives no impression of Dartmoor proper) it is true that the character of the landscape changes markedly as you leave the town.

To the west the road climbs steadily up towards the tourist honeypot of Hay Tor, and the northern route travels past picturesque Lustleigh through the wooded Wray valley to reach Moretonhampstead and the open moorland beyond. The town's other claim to fame is that it is home to the headquarters of the Dartmoor National Park Authority, based at Parke, a splendid house set in spacious parkland just to the west of the town. The River Bovey runs through the National Trust's Parke Estate, and the area provides an excellent range of walking opportunities.

Rails to Trails

The 12-mile (19.3km) Newton Abbot-to-Moretonhampstead railway line was opened in 1866, and finally closed for passenger traffic in 1959. A group of enthusiasts tried to keep it open as a preserved steam line, but were unsuccessful. Attempts are being made at the time of writing to open the line as a walking and cycling route. It was closed for goods traffic to Moretonhampstead in 1964, and to Bovey Tracey in 1970. The line is still laid as track as far as Heathfield, 2 miles (3.2km) south of Bovey Tracey, and is opened to the public on special occasions.

Parke Estate

The building housing the National Park's offices at Parke was built around 1826 on the site of a derelict Tudor house, and left to the National Trust by Major Hole in 1974. In 1999 the eleven National Parks of England and Wales celebrated the 50th anniversary of the legislation that established them. The Dartmoor National Park, covering 368sq miles (953sq km), was number four (in October 1951), following the Peak District, the Lake District and Snowdonia. Walkers should appreciate the purposes behind the National Parks movement – 'the conservation of the natural beauty, wildlife and cultural heritage of the area, and the promotion of the

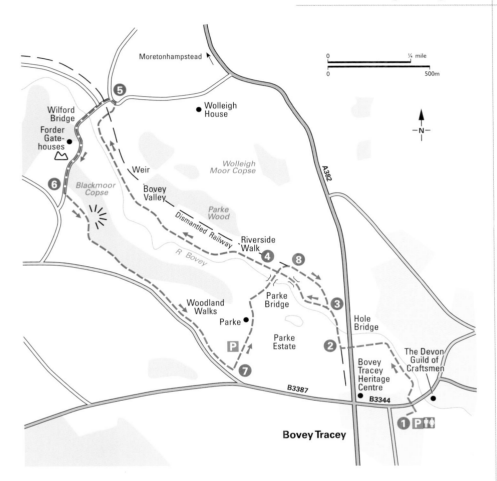

understanding and enjoyment of its special qualities by the public'. The office at Parke is open for enquiries during normal office hours and is a useful port of call before planning any walks on Dartmoor.

RIGHT: Becky Falls in the national park

walk information

➤ **DISTANCE**	3 miles (4.8km)
➤ **MINIMUM TIME**	1hr 30min
➤ **ASCENT/GRADIENT**	196ft (60m) ▲ ▲▲
➤ **LEVEL OF DIFFICULTY**	🚶🚶🚶
➤ **PATHS**	Woodland and field paths, some muddy, 2 stiles
➤ **LANDSCAPE**	Wooded river valley and parkland
➤ **SUGGESTED MAPS**	OS Explorer 110 Torquay & Dawlish
➤ **START/FINISH**	Grid reference: SX 814782
➤ **DOG FRIENDLINESS**	Dogs should be kept under control at all times
➤ **PARKING**	Car park on the B3344 at lower end of Fore Street, Bovey Tracey, with tourist information office (seasonal)
➤ **PUBLIC TOILETS**	At car park

walk directions

1 Cross the road and turn right, following the signs for 'Town centre shops'. Just before you come to the the bridge turn left along a concrete walkway into Mill Marsh Park, past the children's playground and through the arboretum. This level footpath leads past the sports field to meet the busy A382 at Hole Bridge via a kissing gate. Cross the road with care.

2 Go through the kissing gate and turn right to enter the National Trust's Parke Estate on the trackbed of the, now dismantled, Newton Abbot-to-Moretonhampstead railway line. Follow the path over the Bovey.

3 Turn immediately left down wooden steps and through a kissing gate to follow the river. Cross a stile at the field end and continue on a narrow, rough path, high above the river. Descend wooden steps; cross a footbridge into the next field.

4 Parke is over the bridge to the left, and the old railway line is right, but keep ahead through the field into woodland, then go left on a raised wooden walkway to the river. The path winds on, then runs along between woods with fields on the right, then over a footbridge to meet the river at a weir. Keep following the river; eventually two kissing gates lead out of National Trust land. Keep ahead to pass a footbridge over the river left. A little later the footpath bears right to cross the railway track. Turn half left downhill to a lane via a small gate.

5 Turn left (signed 'Manaton') and pass between the old railway bridge piers. Walk across Wilford Bridge, ignoring signs to Lustleigh, right. Continue up the lane past Forder gatehouses, right, then go steeply uphill until the lane bends sharp right.

6 Turn left over a stile to re-enter the Parke Estate. The wooded path is narrow, with views, left over the Bovey Valley. Go through a beech wood and kissing gate to enter a large field. Keep to the right edge, dropping gradually downhill, to leave via a kissing gate and down a narrow wooded path parallel to the road.

7 The path ends at a kissing gate; turn sharp left to walk across the parkland and the drive to Parke car park. Walk downhill to cross the lower drive, then left to go below the house, ending at a five-bar gate. Go through and turn right ('Riverside Walk') to cross the river at Parke Bridge, then ahead to join the old railway track.

8 Turn right and follow the track until it crosses the Bovey, to meet the A382. Cross the road to enter Mill Marsh Park and retrace your steps to your car.

LEFT: *The rocky river bed at Dartmeet*

Through Wanstead Park, where Robert Dudley, the Earl of Leicester, entertained Queen Elizabeth I.

Wanstead and its Royal Connections

ABOVE: The brick-built temple at Wanstead Park is an 18th-century garden house
LEFT: A beautiful bluebell wood in Wanstead Park

The surprising thing about Wanstead Park in east London is that, despite its close proximity to the North Circular road, the distant hum of traffic is really only noticeable from the northern side of the park. This is a lovely walk, enchanting even, for it traces the outline of the ornamental waters and its Grotto and Temple as well as Florrie's Hill. No wonder Elizabeth I returned here again and again.

An Estate Like No Other

Wanstead has been associated with royalty ever since 1553 when Queen Mary, a Roman Catholic, broke her journey here from Norwich to meet her sister, Princess Elizabeth, a Protestant, who rode out to Wanstead accompanied by hundreds of knights on horseback. The estate had belonged to Sir Giles Heron but, because he would not denounce his Catholic beliefs, Henry VIII (the girls' father) took it from him. After Mary's death, Elizabeth became Queen – she was just 25 years old. The estate at Wanstead then belonged to Robert Dudley, the Earl of Leicester, who had enlarged and improved the mansion. The two became very close and Dudley held some extremely lavish parties for his royal guest. In 1578, Elizabeth stayed in Wanstead for five days and no doubt would have spent some time walking in the wonderful grounds.

Highs and Lows

When Queen Elizabeth died, James I succeeded her. In 1607 he spent the autumn in Wanstead. The manor was later sold to Sir James Mildmay. Unfortunately, as Mildmay was one of the judges at the trial of Charles I, which led to Charles' execution, the manor was taken from the family after the restoration and handed to the Crown. In 1667 Sir Josiah Child (whose family were the first private bankers in England) bought the manor and made huge improvements. Later, his son, Sir Richard, replaced the manor house and landscaped the gardens. Constructed using Portland stone, the front of the new mansion had a portico of six Corinthian columns. The building was considered one of the finest in the country, even rivalling Blenheim Palace. The Grotto was erected and the ornamental waters and lakes were also designed at this time. But why, you might ask, is there no mansion today? The blame lies chiefly with Catherine Tilney-Long, who inherited the extremely valuable property in 1794. Despite no shortage of admiring males, she married a gambling man, who took just ten years to blow her entire fortune. To pay off her husband's debts Catherine auctioned the contents of the house and, because a buyer could not be found for the house itself, the magnificent property was pulled down and sold in separate lots. Fortunately for us, despite this sad tale of decline, the wonderful grounds can still be enjoyed.

walk information

➤ **DISTANCE**	4.75 miles (7.7km)	
➤ **MINIMUM TIME**	2hrs 30min	
➤ **ASCENT/GRADIENT**	Negligible	▲ ▲ ▲
➤ **LEVEL OF DIFFICULTY**	🚶🚶🚶	
➤ **PATHS**	Mainly lakeside tracks that can get muddy	
➤ **LANDSCAPE**	Ornamental lake and parkland	
➤ **SUGGESTED MAPS**	OS Explorer 174 Epping Forest & Lee Valley	
➤ **START/FINISH**	Wanstead tube station	
➤ **DOG FRIENDLINESS**	Keep on lead near Kenwood House	
➤ **PUBLIC TOILETS**	By Temple	

walk directions

1 Turn left outside Wanstead tube into The Green, which becomes St Mary's Avenue. At the end cross the road into Overton Drive, which runs to the left of St Mary's Church. After the Bowls and Golf Club turn right, into The Warren Drive. (The building on the right, before the road bends, was once the stable block and coach house to Wanstead House.)

2 At the T-junction turn left and enter Wanstead Park through the gate opposite. Continue ahead downhill (Florrie's Hill) to reach the ornamental water. Follow the path to the left of the water and continue ahead as it runs to the right of the River Roding.

3 After another 0.25 mile (400m) the path swings sharply to the left round an area known as the Fortifications, once a group of eight islands used for storing ammunition used in for duck-shooting and now a bird sanctuary. Soon after this the path traces the outline of a section of the water shaped like a finger. To your left are the steep banks of the River Roding.

4 At a meeting of paths turn right to continue alongside the water. When the path bends to the left, the Grotto can be found ahead.

5 At the T-junction turn right. At the end of the water turn right again, to cross a footbridge; then take the left-hand fork towards grassland. At a crossing of paths keep ahead until you reach a refreshment kiosk. Turn left here and pass beside a barrier on to Northumberland Avenue.

6 Immediately turn right to pick up a path leading to Heronry Pond, which narrows and passes over a mound. At a crossing of paths turn right and then keep ahead across the grass. At the next junction turn sharp right, towards the trees.

7 The path weaves around the pond to reach a barrier. Pass beside this and take a left-hand fork to join a wide, grassy track lined with sweet chestnut trees. At the front of the Temple take the well-defined path on your right. A few paces further on turn left and continue on this path alongside the Temple. Keep ahead at a junction of paths.

8 When you reach the metal enclosure that surrounds the Grotto turn sharp left, as if you are going back on yourself, but, a few paces further on, take a footpath that veers right and hugs the water's edge before joining another, wider path. Turn next left up Florrie's Hill to retrace your steps back to Wanstead tube.

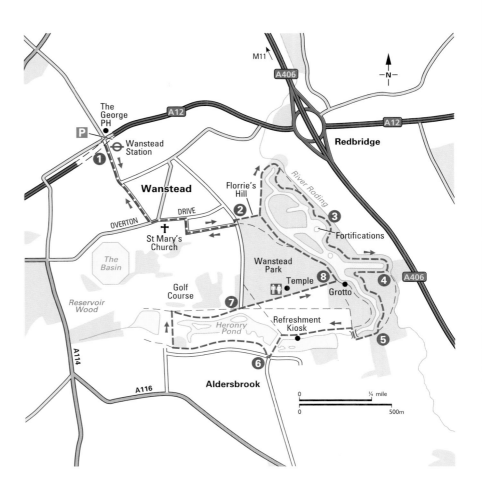

Ancient oaks, historic inclosures and exotic towering conifers in the New Forest.

New Forest Trails

ABOVE: *Dogs should be on a lead on this walk*
LEFT: *Swan Green near Lyndhurst*

A short drive south-west of Lyndhurst are ancient woods of oak and beech, notably Bolderwood, and the impressive, mid-19th-century conifer plantation of the Rhinefield Ornamental Drive. Here you are in the true heart of the New Forest and this fascinating loop walk explores these contrasting landscapes. The shorter loop (the dotted line on the map) is a stroll through the rhododendron-lined Ornamental Drive, with its magnificent tall trees and arboretum, while the longer option takes you through the forest's finest unenclosed and 'inclosed' deciduous woods. Link the two together for a 10-mile (16km) ramble.

Finest Relics of Woodland

Unenclosed woodlands such as Whitley Wood are among the finest relics of unspoiled deciduous forest in Western Europe. Hummocky green lawns and paths meander beneath giant beech trees and beside stands of ancient holly and contorted oaks, and through peaceful, sunny glades edged with elegant silver birch. 'Inclosures' are areas of managed woodlands where young trees are protected from deer and ponies. Areas of oak trees were first inclosed in the late 17th century to provide the huge quantities of timber required by the construction and shipbuilding industries. Holidays Hill Inclosure is one of the forest's oldest, dating from 1676. Here you'll find some 300-year-old oak trees that matured after iron replaced wood in the shipbuilding industry.

You will pass the most famous and probably the oldest tree in the forest, the Knightwood Oak, soon after beginning the longer walk. Believed to be 350 years old, it owes its great age to pollarding (cutting back) its limbs to encourage new branches for fuel and charcoal. Pollarding was made illegal in 1698 as full-grown trees were needed to provide timber for shipbuilding, so any oak or beech tree that show signs of having been pollarded is of a great age. Marvel at the girth of this fine oak, a massive 24ft (7.3m), before walking through Holidays Hill Inclosure.

Close to Millyford Bridge and Highland Water stands the Portugese Fireplace, a memorial to the work of a Portugese Army unit, deployed during the First World War to cut timber for pit-props. The flint fireplace was used in their cookhouse. Returning through Holidays Hill Inclosure you will join a 'reptile trail' and several marker posts, each carved with a different type of British reptile, lead you to the New Forest reptillary. Set up to breed rarer species for the wild, including the smooth snake and sand lizard, it offers you the opportunity to view some of the forest's more elusive inhabitants. Visit on a hot sunny day, when these cold blooded creatures are more active, and you will see the venomous adder, the olive green grass snake, common lizards and the rare natterjack toad.

RIGHT: A quiet path in Rhinefield Ornamental Drive

1 Take the gravel path at the southern end of the car park (beyond the information post), parallel with the road. In 100yds (91m) turn right just before a bench seat and descend to a gravel track. Cross straight over; then, where the path curves left, keep ahead to reach a gate and the A35. Cross over the A35 (take care), go through a gate and keep to the path, uphill to a junction. Turn right and follow the path to Knightwood Oak car park, then follow the sign to the Knightwood Oak itself.

2 Return towards the car park and bear right along the road. Turn right again after a few paces, on to a path into mixed woodland. Cross a stream and soon reach a gravel track. Bear right and keep to this trail, passing red marker posts, to a fork. Keep left to reach a gate and road. Turn right to view the Portuguese Fireplace.

3 Return through Holidays Hill Inclosure to the fork of tracks. Bear left and follow this to the New Forest Reptile Centre. Walk along the access drive past a cottage dated 1811 then, at a barrier on your left, drop down on to a path and follow it across a bridge.

4 Keep to the main path for 0.75 mile (1.2km), skirting the walls to Allum Green and several clearings, then gently climb through trees to a defined crossing of paths and turn right. Shortly, bear half right across a clearing and concrete footbridge, then continue through the woodland edge to an electricity pole. Bear right for 20yds (18m), then left through a gate to the A35.

5 Turn left, then almost immediately right across the road to a gate. Walk ahead to a garden boundary and turn right, the narrow path leading to a lane in Bank. Turn right, pass the Oak Inn and walk through the hamlet.

6 Just beyond the cattle grid, turn right through a gate on to a gravelled track towards Brockenhurst. Follow this track for nearly a mile (1.4km) to a junction at a small green.

7 Fork right towards Brockenhurst, and enter Hursthill Inclosure at a gate. Drop down past a turning on the right, then climb again and bear left at a fork. Keep to the waymarked track as it drops past another turning on the right and leaves Hursthill Inclosure at a gate. Walk the long straight track to the bridge over Highland Water, and follow the track round to the right. Soon a gate leads the waymarked trail into Poundhill Inclosure, and another straight section brings you to a five-way junction at waymark post 24.

8 Turn right here. Ignore all turnings, and follow the track as it turns sharp right and winds its way to a junction with the Ornamental Drive. Turn left for the last 100 yards (91m) back to the car park.

walk information

➤ **DISTANCE**	8 miles (12.9km)
➤ **MINIMUM TIME**	4hrs
➤ **ASCENT/GRADIENT**	318ft (97m)
➤ **LEVEL OF DIFFICULTY**	
➤ **PATHS**	Grass and gravel forest tracks, heathland paths, some roads
➤ **LANDSCAPE**	Ornamental Drive, ancient forest inclosures and heathland
➤ **SUGGESTED MAPS**	OS Explorer OL22 New Forest
➤ **START/FINISH**	Grid reference: SU 266057
➤ **DOG FRIENDLINESS**	Keep dogs under control at all times
➤ **PARKING**	Brock Hill Forestry Commission car park, just off A35
➤ **PUBLIC TOILETS**	Blackwater car park

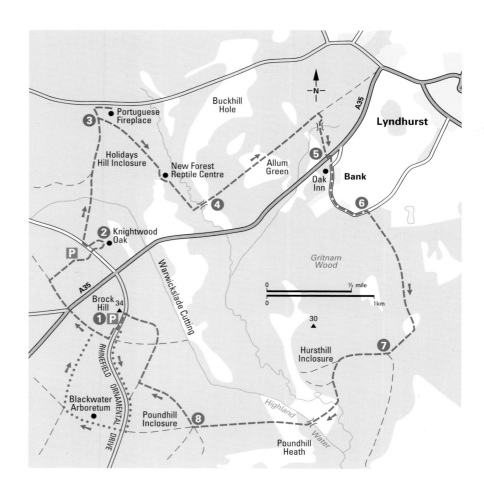

A fine walk with glimpses over the most famous of all the dry chalk valleys.

Devil's Dyke and the World's Grandest View

ABOVE: Looking down the steep-sided Devil's Dyke

Sussex is rich in legend and folklore and the Devil and his fiendish works crop up all over the county. The local landmark of Devil's Dyke is a prime example – perfectly blending the natural beauty of the South Downs with the mystery and originality of ancient mythology. Few other fables in this part of the country seem to have caught the public imagination in quite the same way.

Disturbed by a Candle

Devil's Dyke is a geological quirk, a spectacular, steep-sided downland combe or cleft 300ft (91m) deep and half a mile (800m) long. According to legend, it was dug by the Devil as part of a trench extending to the sea. The idea was to try to flood the area with sea water and, in so doing, destroy the churches of the Weald. However, it seems the Devil might have been disturbed by a woman carrying a candle. Mistaking this for the dawn, he quickly disappeared, leaving his work unfinished. It's a charming tale but the reality of how Devil's Dyke came to be is probably a good deal less interesting. No one knows for sure how it originated, but it was most likely to have been cut by glacial meltwaters when the ground was permanently frozen in the Ice Age.

Rising to over 600ft (180m), this most famous of beauty spots is also a magnificent viewpoint where the views stretch for miles in all directions. The Clayton Windmills are visible on a clear day, as are Chanctonbury Ring, Haywards Heath and parts of the Ashdown Forest. The artist Constable described this view as the grandest in the world.

Devil's Dyke has long been a tourist honeypot. During the Victorian era and in the early part of the 20th century, the place was akin to a bustling theme park with a cable car crossing the valley and a steam railway coming up from Brighton. On Whit Monday 1893 a staggering 30,000 people visited Devil's Dyke. In 1928 HRH the Duke of York dedicated the Dyke Estate for the use of the public forever and in fine weather it can seem just as crowded as it was in Queen Victoria's day. With the car park full and the surrounding downland slopes busy with people simply taking a relaxing stroll in the sunshine, Devil's Dyke assumes the feel of a seaside resort at the height of the season. Hang-gliders swoop silently over the grassy downland like pterodactyls and kite flyers spill from their cars in search of fun and excitement. But don't let the crowds put you off. The views more than make up for the invasion of visitors, and away from the chalk slopes and the car park the walk soon heads for more peaceful surroundings.

Beginning on Summer Down, on the route of the South Downs Way, you drop down gradually to the village of Poynings where there may be time for a welcome pint at the Royal Oak. Rest and relax for as long as you can here because it's a long, steep climb to the Devil's Dyke pub. The last leg of the walk is gentle and relaxing by comparison.

LEFT: A fine early-morning view from the top of Devil's Dyke

walk directions

1 From the Summer Down car park go through the kissing gate and then veer right. Join the South Downs Way and follow it alongside lines of trees. Soon the path curves left and drops down to the road. Part company with the South Downs Way at this point, as it crosses over to join the private road to Saddlescombe Farm, and follow the verge for about 75yds (68m). Bear left at the footpath sign and drop down the bank to a stile.

2 Follow the line of the tarmac lane as it curves right to reach a waymark. Leave the lane and walk ahead alongside power lines, keeping the line of trees and bushes on the right. Look for a narrow path disappearing into the vegetation and make for a stile. Drop down some steps into the woods and turn right at a junction with a bridleway. Take the path running off half left and follow it between fields and a wooded dell. Pass over a stile and continue to a stile in the left boundary. Cross a footbridge to a further stile and now turn right towards Poynings.

3 Head for a gate and footpath sign and turn left at the road. Follow the parallel path along to the Royal Oak and then continue to Dyke Lane on the left. There is a memorial stone here, dedicated to the memory of George Stephen Cave Cuttress, a resident of Poynings for over 50 years, and erected by his widow. Follow the tarmac bridleway and soon it narrows to a path. On reaching the fork, by a National Trust sign for Devil's Dyke, veer right and begin climbing the steps.

4 Follow the path up to a gate and continue up the stairs. From the higher ground there are breathtaking views to the north and west. Make for a kissing gate and head up the slope towards the inn. Keep the Devil's Dyke pub on your left and take the road round to the left, passing a bridleway on the left. Follow the path parallel to the road and look to the left for a definitive view of Devil's Dyke.

5 Head for the South Downs Way and turn left by a National Trust sign for Summer Down to a stile and gate. Follow the trail, keeping Devil's Dyke down to your left, and eventually you reach a stile leading into Summer Down car park.

ABOVE: Villages nestle along the South Downs Way

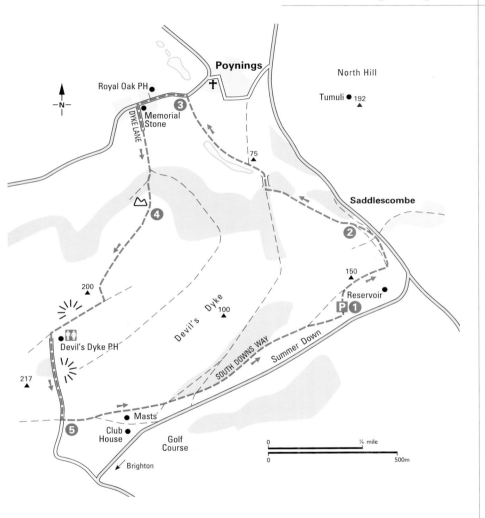

walk information

➤ **DISTANCE**	2.75 miles (4.4km)
➤ **MINIMUM TIME**	1hr 30min
➤ **ASCENT/GRADIENT**	656ft (200m) ▲▲▲
➤ **LEVEL OF DIFFICULTY**	🚶🚶🚶
➤ **PATHS**	Field and woodland paths, 7 stiles
➤ **LANDSCAPE**	Chalk grassland, steep escarpment and woodland
➤ **SUGGESTED MAPS**	OS Explorer 122 Brighton & Hove
➤ **START/FINISH**	Grid reference: TQ 269112
➤ **DOG FRIENDLINESS**	Mostly off lead. On lead on approach to Poynings
➤ **PARKING**	Summer Down free car park
➤ **PUBLIC TOILETS**	By Devil's Dyke pub

Walking in Safety

All these walks are suitable for any reasonably fit person, but less experienced walkers should try the easier walks first. Route finding is usually straightforward, but you will find that an Ordnance Survey map is a useful addition to the route maps and descriptions.

Risks

Although each walk here has been researched with a view to minimising the risks to the walkers who follow its route, no walk in the countryside can be considered to be completely free from risk. Walking in the outdoors will always require a degree of common sense and judgement to ensure that it is as safe as possible.

- Be particularly careful on cliff paths and in upland terrain, where the consequences of a slip can be very serious.
- Remember to check tidal conditions before walking on the seashore.
- Some sections of route are by, or cross, busy roads. Take care and remember traffic is a danger even on minor country lanes.
- Be careful around farmyard machinery and livestock, especially if you have children with you.
- Be aware of the consequences of changes in the weather and check the forecast before you set out. Carry spare clothing and a torch if you are walking in the winter months. Remember the weather can change very quickly at any time of the year, and in moorland and heathland areas, mist and fog can make route finding much harder. Don't set out in these conditions unless you are confident of your navigation skills in poor visibility. In summer remember to take account of the heat and sun; wear a hat and carry spare water.
- On walks away from centres of population you should carry a whistle and survival bag. If you do have an accident requiring the emergency services, make a note of your position as accurately as possible and dial 999.

Acknowledgements

The Automobile Association would like to thank the following photographers, companies and picture libraries for their assistance in the preparation of this book.

Abbreviations for the picture credits are as follows: (t) top; (b) bottom; (l) left; (r) right; (AA) AA World Travel Library.

2/3 AA/T Mackie; 5 AA/T Mackie; 6 AA/D Hall; 7bl AA/M Kipling; 7bcl AA/T Mackie; 7bcr AA/S Day; 7br AA/T Mackie; 10/11 AA/T Mackie; 12 AA/J Morrison; 12/13 AA/L Whitwam; 15 AA/M Kipling; 16 AA/ M Kipling; 17 AA/L Whitwam; 18 AA/A Whitwam; 19 AA/L Whitwam; 21 AA/L Whitwam; 22 AA/M Kipling; 22/23 AA/S&O Mathews; 25 AA/G Rowatt; 26/27 AA/T Mackie; 27 AA/E A Bowness; 28/29 AA/P Sharpe; 29 AA/E A Bowness; 30 AA/A Mockford & N Bonetti; 32 AA/T Mackie; 32/33 AA/T Mackie; 34 AA/E A Bowness; 35 AA/ S Day; 37 AA/T Mackie; 38/39 AA/T Mackie; 39 AA/E A Bowness; 40 AA/A Mockford & N Bonetti; 40/41 AA/T Mackie; 42 AA/T Mackie; 44 AA/M Birkitt; 45 AA/T Mackie; 48/49 AA/T Mackie; 49 AA/ A J Hopkins; 52 AA/T Mackie; 52/53 AA/T Mackie; 56/57 AA/T Mackie; 57 AA/T Mackie; 60/61 AA/T Mackie; 61 AA/T Souter; 62/63 AA/ T Mackie; 64 AA/T Mackie; 65 AA/T Mackie; 66/67 AA/S Day; 67 AA/ D Hall; 68 AA/H Palmer; 69 AA/D Hall; 71 AA/H Palmer; 72 AA/ K Doran; 72/73 AA/S Day; 74 AA/S Day; 76 AA/S Day; 76/77 AA/ S Day; 78/79 AA/S Day; 79 AA/K Doran; 81 AA/F Stephenson; 82 AA/R Ireland; 82/83 AA/P Baker; 84 AA/R Ireland; 85 AA/M Jourdan; 86 AA/R Ireland; 87 AA/R Moss; 88 AA/C Jones; 90/91 AA/A Lawson; 92/93 AA/A Lawson; 93 AA; 94 AA/C Jones; 96/97 AA/P Baker; 98/99 Nic Hamilton/Alamy; 99 AA/L Hatts; 102/103 AA/P Baker; 103 AA/ T Souter; 105 AA/A Burton; 107 AA/J Miller; 108/109 AA/J Miller; 110/111 AA/J Miller

Every effort has been made to trace the copyright holders, and we apologise in advance for any accidental errors. We would be happy to apply the corrections in the following edition of this publication.